A Year in a Yurt

A Year in a Yurt

Autumn and Adam Raven

Published 2012 by Autumn Writing

Book design by Autumn Writing

Copyright © 2016 Autumn Raven

Cover art by Autumn and Adam Raven

ISBN: 1535028661

ISBN-13: 978-1535028660

DISCOVER OTHER TITLES BY
AUTUMN AND ADAM RAVEN
INCLUDING:

CONTENTS

INTRODUCTION

"A yurt is elemental. Wood and fabric around air, it breathes with the wind. Round, it treats all directions equally. Traditionally, the center is sacred. Sunlight pours in through the center dome, marking time and seasons as the light crosses the floor. Sound is not shut out by the thin walls. You hear the best and worst: traffic, planes, shouting, music of a passing car versus the wind, the gentlest of rain, the pounding of storms, jolts of thunder, the whisper of snow falling across the roof. I know the weather before I open my eyes."

- Autumn: 6 March 2011

I f you do not know what a yurt is, do not worry. I've only met a number shy of a dozen who knew what a yurt was and were not overtly surprised by my choice of lodging even in the rural state of Maine. The yurt is one of the oldest forms of habitation and it is still in use today. Known as a ger in its native home of Mongolia, yurts have existed for centuries. Before the time of Christ, before the Buddha, people were living in gers.

These original gers, and their modern descendants still used on the windswept Mongolian landscape, were made with wooden frames and felted wool coverings. Insulation was another blanket added to the wall. Air conditioning was rolling up the outer covering. Some designs used doors, others a hanging flap which was often elaborately decorated.

What has become known as a yurt began to take shape in the 1960's. At a small school in New Hampshire, Bill Coperthwaite, who taught about indigenous cultures, put his mathematics class to work. What came out was a new design for a ger-type structure. The idea touched many people. Designs developed along with companies over the years until finally the western version of a yurt had become standardized into three forms: fabric walled, frame paneled, and tapered walled. All use modern materials such as steel aircraft cable, NASA designed insulation, architectural fabrics, and treated woods.

Yurts are subtle. For something so unlike a traditional stick built home, they do not stand out unless designed to do so. Like their owners, many fade into the background merging with woodlands and fields. They are a quiet place and have a different feel compared to an average modern house. Or they are a place that asks for quiet and sounds, once taken for granted, become an intrusion.

Perhaps that is why there has been a surge in the popularity of yurts as structures for backcountry huts and campgrounds. Yurts are now designed and found from the tropics to Alaska, from Mongolia to Europe, to the Americas and back around to Japan. They are used as rental structures due to their mobility and strength, temporary homes for people in transition, and as permanent dwellings.

Size wise, they can be tiny secluded huts or mobile camping yurts a mere ten to twelve feet across. Or they can soar to multi-story marvels 100 feet across. The average size for fabric yurts seems to be in the 20 to 30-foot diameter, providing a modest 500 to 700 square feet of living space akin to micro-apartments found in many cities. Space, and the ability to make the most of it through multi-purpose furniture, is highly prized. As is sheer simplicity.

Round, the yurt heritage is from sacred structures so that they come imbued with a sense of the extraordinary even if the owner does not share the ideology or culture of the ger's inception. Four directions rolled together and the sacred center open to sky, a year spent in a yurt opens the occupant to a reconnection with nature, time of day, and seasons of the year. Especially in a fabric walled yurt. It is inevitable when your abode is a very large four-season tent.

A yurt is many things. For me, it has become home.

— Autumn

WHY A YURT?
LIFE UP TO MARCH 31, 2010

"I feel trapped. Most of my paycheck goes to either the mortgage or things we need to keep the house maintained. My weekends go to the gardens, painting, cleaning all the rooms. And there is so much more that needs to be done and fixed. It just isn't fun anymore."

- Autumn: 15 August 2009

"It all comes down to money. I would say time and money, but there are formulas to figuring out how valuable my time is even at home. I have longer remaining on our mortgage than I have until retirement. On this schedule, I'll never be free to follow my dreams. I'll be too busy paying off the American one."

- Autumn: 4 October 2009

W e were in debt. Perhaps not as bad as my husband and I once had been, but in debt nonetheless. Many people have asked why we did this. Why would we sell our home, car, ATV, snowmobile, furniture, why donate over 90% of our belongings and move into a yurt, in Maine no less? I keep coming back to the answer of finances and especially debt.

Owing money is an obligation. It tied me down with a promise to be steady and responsible, to take care of what was owed even if it meant sacrificing my dreams. Besides, chucking it all to go pursue crazy desires was a sign of immaturity. Wasn't it? Or was it the sole reason for living?

This is a question that is difficult to answer. What I could wrap my head around was that I owed money on the house and to credit cards. Most of my paycheck went to bills, most of which went to pay off creditors or to support the maintenance of the thing that we owed the most money on: the house. That burden kept me from imagining what other realities might exist. I, we, were stuck.

No change happens without a beginning. There is no birth without conception and no conception without love. So it is that I cannot pinpoint the moment that led up to the yurt even though I can mark the day that Adam presented me with the idea: March 27, 2010.

The yurt came after the decision to sell the house. What we were going to do if the house sold was a topic not really discussed. It was too frightening, too exciting. And the idea of selling the house was only a glimmer during the three years prior to that decision while we got rid of the excess of belongings with which we'd filled every nook and cranny of our traditional home. The purge of goods came before the thought of selling. And the expulsion of excess belongings came after a revelation of how much money we lost due to interest rates on credit cards. The first decision that set off the domino chain was to get out of debt. That was nearly five years before I'd ever considered a yurt as a potential home.

I was away at a conference, one on which my husband accompanied me. We checked the bank account and realized that we had no money. Here we were in a destination city and the only way we could do anything was to charge it. Of course, we'd charged his extra ticket. The credit cards were tight as well. Sitting and listening to session after session of the conference, my brain started to whirl. This wasn't how I had envisioned my adult life. This wasn't the life I wanted.

Debt hadn't just happened. My husband and I were responsible for the situation in which we found ourselves. We would also have to be the solution. Some serious discussions ensued. Adam took over the long-term financial planning. Up until that point, I'd paid the bills and he'd been rather divorced from how we were really doing. With both of us involved, things quickly began to improve. First we stopped using the credit cards.

As financial organization ensued, so did physical. Why did we have so much stuff? The very things that had gotten us into debt lay scattered about the house and were rarely used. What had we been thinking to buy such and such? So began the period of the great donation. We cleaned out the eaves, the basement, and most of the garage until everything you saw was all we owned. All the while, we bought less, used what we had, and paid off first one credit card then another. Then we kept going.

The clutter went next. As did the home equity loan, rolled into a new mortgage with lower interest rates. We were beginning to feel a bit of financial freedom. Somewhere in there, I switched jobs and no longer had an hour-plus commute one way to work. I spent more time at home, looking at the remains of my hobbies pushed aside to better cope with long workdays and the maintenance our 200-plus-year-old chestnut timber frame cape with its fieldstone foundation and dirt floor basement required, and I wondered why I was so in love with the place.

Our little historic cape

Were we not constantly wishing that something could be changed such as the slanted floors or the oddly made fireplace? To fix our aged home would take money, a lot of money. More than the house was worth, really. Not to mention the time I spent on it. Every weekend seemed a new odyssey of repairs, maintenance, or cleaning. Sunday evenings rolled around when I hoped to have a few hours to pursue one of my former favorite pastimes, writing to drawing to simply sitting and reading. I was usually too tired to do anything other than dread work the next day. I was starting to really not like being home.

I did love a lot about that house: the massive kitchen, the sunny back yard, the woods that took up most of the six acres. I had just spent over a month using the jigsaw on the old custom made pine cabinets in the kitchen to build a spice shelf and wine rack. Then I painted the stained knotty pine to espresso white and misty green.

My favorite spot though was the sunporch. We'd put a lot of work into finishing it with new tiled floors and two French doors, one of which involved using a tiger saw to install an exterior wall. The room faced south and had ten skylights as well as triple hung windows that looked out to the backyard and forest beyond. It was full of light barely framed by a house.

One side of the sunporch – the other contained screens

Spanning the whole length of the cape, the sunporch was over 30 feet long and 15 feet wide. We spent most of our time there. Then it dawned on us that we could live in the sun porch, or at least something that size. We looked once more around at our Norman-Rockwell-would-love-it 2,000-square-foot cape and put it on the market.

This was in 2009. We didn't have our hopes up for a quick sell, but we didn't need to sell either. No matter what the market is like, it takes a unique individual to want to own a 200- year-old house. This one had uneven pinewood floors that squeaked, and a narrow second-floor living space where the bedrooms were located. You could barely stand in them due to the low ceiling. At least we'd put in a new septic, an upgrade from the cesspool with which the house had come. And the one and only bathroom was modern as well as most of the house wiring. So we really weren't worried about the market. There was a charm to the house with its spacious kitchen, sunporch, a modern two-car garage, all wrapped together on a quiet road. We just needed someone else crazy enough to see it.

We continued to separate belongings into things to keep versus those to give away or sold. Then we realized that we needed to clear out the house in case it did sell. We bought a ten-foot by 16-foot pre-built shed and placed it on Adam's family's land. Now we had storage with no monthly fee and a place to put those things we wanted to keep without having them underfoot. Plus, it limited us in how much we could keep.

Two lookie loos came during the fall that we put the house on the market and then winter fell across Maine. Houses don't sell in the winter up here. It is just too difficult to tell what you are buying. So for us, the packing and worry about selling fell away as the snow buried Maine.

In the early spring of 2010, Adam and I were immersed in plans. I had a weeklong conference and training in Kansas City and Adam had purchased a 1981 BMW R80 G/S motorcycle in New Mexico. He was heading out on a one-way ticket to pick it up, fix it, and ride it back. If all went well, he could make it back in two weeks. He was hoping to meet me in Kansas City on the way back east, stop at my parents' in Pennsylvania, and then have a quick shot to Maine in early spring - cold and snowy? - weather. Needless to say, we considered his adventure an open ended odyssey.

The R80 G/S outfitted for a trip

Adam was in New Mexico with his new motorcycle in pieces due to a blown rear main oil seal. The house was in tatters from a winter of "just put it inside until the snow melts," Adam's packing for a trip full of unknowns, and me packing for a week away. I was three days away from my flight south when the realtor called me. Of course, someone wanted to come and see the house. The first of the spring hunters. I groaned.

I was up until 11 p.m. cleaning. They would come in the late afternoon on Friday. Afterward I would go home, finish packing and shut up the house to leave Sunday morning. Impatient, I gave them an hour and a half before finally heading home, only to meet both the realtors and a pleasant couple still dawdling in the driveway. I answered their questions, apologized to the realtors, and proceeded to get my stuff together.

I heard from my realtor on Saturday. The couple was going to submit an offer on the house on Sunday. I was more annoyed than excited. I altered my packing to include my laptop and a cell modem, happy that my realtor could at least email offers to me as I headed out of state.

I got the first offer while on a layover in Chicago's O'Hare. I fired back a counteroffer and ran for my plane. So began a week of back and forth during every break of my conference along with several calls to my realtor in the evenings. By week's end, Adam had joined me in Kansas City. The final negotiations fell into place and we had a moment to sit and chat. Did we really want to sell the house? If we did, what to do next?

I had been thinking of renting an apartment. But with our two small dogs and even with our downsized possessions, the idea was daunting. As Adam continued his journey northeast alone, he had to confront our altered reality. Gone was the idea of restoring the motorcycle in the two-car garage. We had just agreed to sell the house and garage. Soon, if everything went well, we would own only a shed full of boxes and two cars. During all of our planning to get out of debt, reduce what we owned and sell the house, we'd never really explored the next step. This was what Adam had to consider as he crossed the prairie chased by a brewing snowstorm hissing at the heels of his motorcycle boots.

Adam thought about a houseboat. He knew about my love of water and that one of my greatest desires was to live in a home on the water that rose and fell with the tide. But Maine has many challenges, not the least of which is no access to pump stations for most of the fall, winter, and spring. A houseboat was not practical if we had to dump septic waste into the sea, even if it was legal, because neither one of us felt right about it, particularly in the middle of winter when getting far enough from shore was a big enough challenge.

Adam's mother had recently returned from a trip to Mongolia. Somewhere in the vast expanse of the plains with a spring snowstorm sending tendrils of icy flurries towards him connected with the images his mother had brought home. It brewed in his mind until the thought emerged: Why not a yurt?

By the time he found his way back to Maine, the idea had bloomed into a plan. As we packed boxes one day, he turned to me. "I have this crazy idea ..." So begins many of Adam's proposals. I knew what a yurt was because I had met people through work that had lived in a "yome," another name often used for yurts. I knew of the concept. But the living arrangements and benefits of moving into a giant tent were another matter.

My challenge to my husband? Show me what you are talking about. Up came pictures of yurt interiors via the internet. Rafters rising to the center dome, the lattice criss-crossing sun- flooded windows, the possibilities of kitchens and bathrooms were alluring.

A simple home that we could configure how we liked with a little work and some wood.

Visually, I was not against the yurt concept, but that was just one item on the list. Adam's research paid off as he outlined how a yurt was insulated: a thin NASA designed layer akin to bubble wrap between two sheets of aluminum foil. We talked about heaters, wood stoves, kitchens, composting toilets, solar panels, where to put it, and finally cost.

A new 24-foot yurt would cost around $13,000. Add a few thousand more for a deck to set it on and we'd be out $20,000. It was an amount that without a mortgage and with some concentrated effort, we could pay off in under two years. Maybe even one. That thought alone was enough to make me bite. No monthly rental payment, a loss that could never be recouped? No 30-year mortgage on which the payoff seemed a chimera? Adam's parents had offered us a small lot on their 16-acre property, a move of a mere two miles from our current house. Plus they were willing to provide us a family loan for the yurt.

Oddly enough, the potential income savings wasn't the biggest argument. Nor was it the vision of being able to design and build an interior, something that my crafty nature jumped on with full force. Instead it was Adam's soft voice talking about how much we'd enjoyed our camping motorcycle trip the summer before. We'd lived outside for 16 days except for three nights in hotels. We'd loved every minute of it. Vacations had always been a time of peace, a chance to slow down and enjoy being outdoors. With only the gear we could carry on two motorcycles, we'd been fine and comfortable. A yurt, the financial freedom it could offer, and the chance to simplify while living in a way we enjoyed was an opportunity I could not pass up. In the end, a yurt as a future home was agreed to without much debate. Of course, first we needed the house sale to go through.

—Autumn

"What the hell are we going to live in? Houseboat?
Sure, that would be nice during a nor'easter in Maine.
Rental? Nah. Paying rent to some greedy landlord and living
next to another renter with a big dog is not practical. A
yurt...? Yeah that might work, once I figure out what the hell
it is."

- Adam: March 15th 2009, while riding through Ohio

Seems that after living the dream, the American Dream, for so long you tend to forget something: your own dreams. You know those crazy ideas you had as a kid? The ones that people said you'd grow out of? The ones of you taking a boat and sailing across the ocean, or exploring unseen lands. Yeah, those dreams that you are supposed to forget in order to be an adult. Sorry world, it never happened to me.

I've been rather fortunate in life. Sure I've done some of the 9-5, but honestly I've always had a safety net. At least I thought I did until I realized that the net was supported by high interest credit cards and bank loans. Once I took over the long-term financial planning, I came to realize the implications of ignoring the pennies on the sidewalk. One hundred pennies is a dollar, one thousand is ten, and seventy-five thousand was equivalent to what we were giving away to a single credit card company in one month. Do the math, multiply that by three, then add the mortgage. Life had to change.

Life did change once we learned how to manage our pennies. Budgets were hammered out, bills were minimized, and in some cases eliminated. Better rates were negotiated. Tax strategies were sought out to maximize returns to help pay off debt. After a few years we were down to one last thing: the house.

A house, rather a mortgage, is not something you can simply pay some extra on for a few years, kick a few tax returns towards, and get it paid off. Well, actually you can if you make a good income and drop a LOT of it towards principle, but that was not our situation. Ours was a single income, spending what we could on the house, and it did not work for our life goals. The decision was made to shoot the big cash hungry hippo: sell the house and free ourselves.

Fast forward nine months, I'm negotiating to buy a project bike in New Mexico. I figured it had been a few years since I got anything for myself, and the trip sounded like an adventure. Everything was paid off but the house, and it would be a good reward for all the years of saving and budgeting. I flew down in March and picked it up. Ten miles from the seller's house, it broke down.

Omen? Nah, a test of resiliency. The delay allowed me to experience a part of the country I had never seen before: Madrid, Santa Fe, Albuquerque. A splendid state with wonderful people.

One thing that did strike a cord was how they lived. The houses were mud brick adobes with very thick walls. They were warm and draft free, yet cool in the heat of the summer. The houses also seemed to blend in with the surroundings to become a part of nature, rather than dominating it as is common back east. I eventually got the bike fixed and running and headed out to rendezvous with Autumn a thousand miles away in Kansas City at her conference. Eventually I arrived having fought snow, cold rain and hypothermia. I finally got there only to be told that the house had a sale offer. Where the hell was the bike going to go ...?

The garage – where Adam had hoped to rebuild the R80 G/S

Once thawed out I realized I had to come up with a plan and fast. For the remainder of the trip, I tossed around many ideas ranging from a converted metal container, to a micro-house, and I finally thought about a yurt. The problem was ... I had no damn idea what the hell a yurt was. I knew it was a tent ... but seriously, a tent in winter? It wasn't until I got to a computer that night that the idea started to take shape...

I had a planned stop at Autumn's parents' where I had an interesting conversation with her mom. The drift: I'd better provide a good home for their daughter. Oh boy! They are going to LOVE the yurt idea!!!

So there you have it: debt lost, a dead hippo, and some really annoyed in-laws.

— Adam

HOUSE SALE AND PRE-CONSTRUCTION
APRIL & MAY 2010

"I was ambivalent about selling the house until we thought of the yurt and the freedom from a mortgage and monthly bills it could give us. Now I'm so afraid the sale won't go through. What if the buyer backs out? What if the inspection comes back with tons of problems? What if the appraisal is too low?"

- Autumn: 30 March 2010

There was too much to pack to waste much time. The buyer wanted to close on the house on May 14th. That gave us a little over a month and a half by the calendar to clear it out. Adding to the pressure was a week at the end of May when I was scheduled to attend another conference. As luck would have it, I had a long dreamed of vision correction surgery scheduled for no other than May 14th — in Canada. Even with all the years of casting off excess possessions, the timeline looked daunting.

Yet there was a strange inertia as well. With a horrible housing market and frequent warnings of appraisals coming in too low, not to mention what an inspection would find on a 200-year-old house, part of us just didn't believe the sale was going to go through. We lived in a state of half-packed boxes and anxiety.

The report from the home inspection, which took place while Adam and I were both still on the road in March, came back first. The verdict was surprisingly benign: a dry rotted timber located in the dirt floor basement and some suggestions on how to dry out said basement. Beyond a snippy back and forth over the buyer not liking our current wood stove and us saying, "Tough, we aren't buying you a new one," the sale was still on. We packed a few more boxes and got a quote on a yurt.

The more I thought about the yurt, the more the idea kept growing on me. What sort of kitchen would I build? The creation of the wine rack and spice shelves in our current house gave me the confidence to think I could build whatever I wanted. I'd always liked to work in wood, but had only dabbled with odds and ends. Now I was toying with the idea of constructing my home. The yurt would not come pre-assembled. I was getting truly hooked on the idea. Which made the wait for the appraisal all the harder.

We weren't trying to make a profit on the sale of the house. In an ideal world with all the work we'd put into the cape, we could have paid for the whole yurt and been debt free within a few months. Instead, we were just holding on to hope by our fingernails that we could break even. The plan was to walk away from our old life and begin a new, simpler one with a focus on staying out of debt and saving some cash. This grew from a dim light to dreams of retiring early or taking a break mid-career to see a few things best traversed while young enough to take the risks involved.

The appraisal came in the afternoon of April 9th. It was so close. Our future was caught in the difference of a mere $6,000. Without it, we wouldn't be able to pay off the mortgage. I felt breathless with a thousand ants crawling over me. The buyer had already proven himself stubborn. He wouldn't pay anything additional out-of-pocket. The sale had to be through a mortgage and the bank wouldn't lend more than the house was worth.

We argued with the bank and appraisal companies. The 'comps' they had come up with were hardly comparable and, of course, did not favor our asking price. Nothing like a 200-year-old cape on a pretty dead-end road had sold in the last two years. The appraisal company listened, reviewed their paperwork, and made no changes. I couldn't believe the whole thing would come apart on so little of a difference.

It was our realtor who came up with the solution. She offered to take only 4% commission if the other realtor would agree to the reduction as well. There was some hesitation on the other realtor's part, but eventually he agreed. We learned later that the buyer offered to cover the 2% reduction to his realtor outside of the sale. So much for no cash on hand to put towards the house. A new sale agreement was drafted. The buyer signed. So did we. It was now mid-April and we had one month to pack the house, buy a yurt, and build a deck to put it on. Meanwhile, it was one of the busiest times of the year at my full-time job plus I had a one-week conference coming up, as well as preparation for an office review during the first week in June, right after coming back from eye surgery and putting up the yurt. If all went well.

We were spastic. Adam, originally planning on attending the conference with me, stayed home to pack and work with a contractor we'd hired to build a platform for the yurt. Ideally, we would have built the deck ourselves, but with three weeks to go until the sale there just wasn't time. The contractor would cost more, but could get the job done. Adam would make sure of that.

Deck construction ran a gamut of problems. The site we'd chosen was on a steep hillside. Although one edge of the deck would be only a foot off the ground, the opposite corner was tall enough to drive the Jeep under. During the week I was gone, Adam contended with footings hitting bedrock ledge a foot below the soil surface, a mixed snow/hailstorm, and keeping costs reasonable. By the first of May and my return, a lofty framework spanned the hillside. We'd planned a platform that was 30 feet by 35 feet with the yurt to be placed at one corner, leaving a large deck space in front.

By the end of the following week, the remaining decking was installed and the higher yurt platform insulated and covered with floor-grade plywood. The costs for the deck kept inching upwards as we realized how tight our timeline was running. Did we have time to build the railings we'd envisioned? Not really, but it was best to have something rather than nothing. We paid to have the railings and stairs off the back to the "driveway" constructed as well. We barely had time to check the progress much less worry about all the details. The deck looked solid enough. Any doubts surfaced around two in the morning and were quickly buried.

We jokingly referred to the deck project as a helicopter landing pad

We ordered the yurt on May 2nd, too excited to wait until the house sale went though. We bought from Pacific Yurts, an established company with a good reputation. We wanted to be sure if there were any problems, the company we bought from would still be around in the future. Or if we needed a new side cover or dome, we could buy replacement parts. It was an exciting moment to schedule delivery for June 4th. It was also nerve racking to realize we'd built a deck and ordered a yurt, spending over $20,000 of borrowed money and we still owned a house. The slight chance of the sale somehow falling through became an obsession.

I don't remember much of the last week of owning our little cape. Every moment at home was spent packing or tossing. We had a dumpster brought in which we filled to the brim. The rush to leave pushed aside most of our recycle and reuse consciousness as we scrambled to keep the sale on schedule.

The buyer wanted some railroad ties we'd use for driveway edging removed. We advertised in Uncle Henry's, a local listing for want ads, for someone to take all of them for $25. In one day they were gone. I left cans of the paint that matched the floors and cabinets, replacement windows, anything I thought that belonged to the house in the basement. We were soon to be just another one of its long list of previous owners in the epic life of a very old house.

I began to see the realtors as akin to divorce lawyers. They relayed messages from the buyer to us and back again, altering the language to something less offensive. Word that the buyer wanted some object moved or removed would come from my realtor with an apology. My epitaphs would return to him with soothing expressions that it would be done. A tree that had fallen in the forest near the lawn was removed and other items were pointed out as not actually on the property so they couldn't be touched. A debate on whether the garage had been listed as heated and if it had a wood stove or a heater became a duel of carefully worded menace. When it came right down to it we were frazzled and running out of time. I started leaving work early if I could, and took a day off whenever possible.

The garage during the move

Then the fact that we had to leave on Thursday, May 13th came up. My surgery was for the afternoon of May 14th and I needed to be "well rested" if it was to be successful. With a closing plus an eight-hour drive, well rested didn't fit the bill for leaving on the 14th. The word from the buyer was that our "little run to Canada seemed suspicious." That left us stumped. Did he think we were running out on selling the house? Our realtor scratched her head, shrugged, and thankfully made arrangements for us to sign the closing papers the day before. Now my eye surgery had a bonus, we wouldn't have to sit across from our very demanding buyers at closing. I was thoroughly grateful.

As we approached the sale, our once careful cataloging of everything that went into a box, something we'd started when we'd begun clearing the house out over a year before, dropped to such descriptions as 'misc. kitchen.' The stress finally became too much for Adam. It culminated in a horrible intestinal upset. The last night in the house, the night of May 12th, was very bad. With everything removed except a futon, a few boxes, and what we needed during the week in Canada required for my eye surgery, the house was more than empty. It was cold.

I'd left just enough blankets and pillows to make it through the night. Adam was so sick, he couldn't sleep in bed. Stomach cramps and the frequent need for the toilet kept him thrashing. He ended up 'sleeping' on the floor of the bathroom upstairs. I knew he was cold. He was sick, feverish and shaking. I took him all but one pillow and the sheet. Making sure he was as comfortable as he could be in a nest of the comforter and pillows, I went back downstairs and wrapped the remaining sheet around myself as many times as possible. I knew if I fell asleep, I'd be fine. I tend to heat up while snoozing. I lay in the dark listening to the old house creak, fighting off the cold, hoping I wouldn't get sick as well, and just wanting the whole ordeal to be over.

We were to be at the lawyer's office at 11 o'clock. After that, we were heading to Canada. It didn't even come close to happening. What we thought would be one minor haul down the road kept growing as we found more and more misplaced and nearly forgotten items. In the end, we raced to the lawyer's office, and signed the papers under the watchful eyes of a legal team and our realtor, who kept telling us everything would be fine and not to worry. After that, we went back to the house and continued throwing together the last items. We didn't take the final load to Adam's parents' house until three in the afternoon. Exhausted and with an eight-hour drive to Canada still ahead of us, we turned the car north, making sure we had our passports and rabies certificates for the two dogs.

**Most trips to the storage were made with a Jeep
and a trailer**

Even at that point, the deal still nearly fell through. Moments after we pulled out of the yard, the buyer pulled in for his last walk-through. He was not pleased. An admitted misunderstanding from his realtor had left a few large logs in a right-of-way adjacent to our property. The buyer wanted them gone. The paint left in sealed cans that matched the walls in the house, a few boards of usable lumber, and other items too minor and innumerable to mention, needed to be removed. Otherwise, he would hold back $5,000 from the sale. An amount that meant our mortgage would not be closed.

By now we were across the border in New Brunswick talking on a cell phone to our realtor. "Don't worry," she told me. "I can take care of it. Everything will be set for closing."

I was in tears, Adam was between delirious and trying not to throw up. So much for being well rested for my surgery. Somehow our realtor convinced us not to turn around. To this day, I don't know how she did it, who she called, or really how much needed to be done. I've heard that she was there until 11 p.m. that night and back again the next day before the closing for one final walk-through. Adam and I both knew we owed the sale actually going through to our realtor. Years after that day and I still cannot fully express my gratitude for what she did, far beyond her duties as a realtor. She did not even charge us for all the extra time and work. Nor has she ever made it seem like we owed her a penny or hour of service in kind.

While our realtor slaved away on a house that we'd left far better and far emptier than we had bought it, Adam and I checked into our hotel in Canada. He found the bathroom, I sat shaking on the bed too exhausted to be worried. Which was good. The next morning would bring, hopefully, the sale of the house. But my mind was finally turning toward the fairly invasive eye surgery. I fell asleep wondering what I'd gotten myself into.

—Autumn

*"Stewart Little, that no good rotten piece of weasel shit
can rot in hell for all I care. I hate that man, I hate that
man, I hate that man ... I hope the house collapses on him"*
- Adam remarking on the buyer of our house after
one more of many paltry demands: April 2010

The deck construction provided an interesting experience. We decided that, as the yurt was not entirely permanent, we wished to make the deck mobile as well. This would include screwing the deck boards and bolting the structural beams together. In hindsight, this is actually how decks are supposed to be constructed minus the ability to disassemble the sub-framing.

Our goal was also to stay under a set budget. Finding someone to meet these requirements proved challenging. For one thing we wished to build the yurt on the side of a hill with one side a foot off the ground and the far side eight feet in the air. Many contractors looked at the idea and declined as they felt the deck needed to be engineered. Despite the short time frame and needing to pack the house, we considered, reluctantly, building it ourselves.

It happened that my parents were having a local husband and wife team do some construction on their home and suggested that we have them look at our project. I'll refer to the team as the Illuminati. They seemed nice and felt they could tackle it. The Illuminati gave an estimate of $9,000 for the work. We had no idea about deck construction and since it needed to be done in three weeks, we figured it was a fair price.

The first day of construction and during materials delivery, it started to snow and ice. Cold set in and made an ominous start of things to come. I'd been told by the contractors that if I assisted them the price would be considerably lower. Despite everything that needed to be completed packing the house, I thought this was a fair trade and spent the next three weeks working with them as much as I could.

The first step was to create a foundation. The Illuminati strongly recommended friends who installed a product called techno-posts, which are basically drilled metal poles that reach below frost-line, and could be embedded when ledge was hit. $2500 later we had several fancy green posts to build the deck on.

The initial stages of building the deck included the framework which was comprised of eight by eight-inch pressure-treated wooded beams, spaced four across, and nailed, not bolted, together. Then came the two by eight sixteen-inch on center spaced flooring joists, once again nailed not screwed together. Finally the center circle on which the yurt would be built was constructed.

Tech-no-post poles supporting the initial deck framing

Mind you, in the quote for the estimate we'd asked for a platform that could be disassembled. I kept reminding the Illuminati about this. They pointed to the issue of speed if they used a nailgun, which would save us money. Screws and sinking each one would take time and cost more. With construction started and time moving quickly, we were at an impasse. The platform became a permanent structure.

The yurt platform was a 24-foot circle with insulation, flooring, and a strip of marine grade plywood encircling it that also had to be a quarter inch higher that the flooring for attaching the yurt lattice walls. Explaining this to the Illuminati was a challenge to say the least. We told them we needed a floor and had plans, but it needed to be removable as well. We'd relented on the deck being made permanent. After all, my parents could use it if we moved, but the yurt platform needed to go with the yurt.

Foam insulation going in the yurt platform

Their answer to our needs started with standard household insulation for the floor. Then they set up a table saw to cut blue polystyrene two-inch thick insulation into strips ... while spreading the not-too-environmentally-friendly shavings throughout the neighborhood. The strips were laid into the floor cavity and glued in place with liquid nails. Once it was fully insulated, three-quarter-inch flooring was cut and, not screwed, but both glued and nailed down excessively with glue impregnated nails to make sure everything stayed put.

Once the yurt foundation was complete, the Illuminati started on the decking. Out came the nail gun again. By now I was exasperated. I reminded them once more about the necessity for disassembly later. They asked me if I wanted to pay more. When I told them $9K was already high, they said they had to use nails, but not as big as necessary. We should be able to pry them out. Screwing, however, would take them almost a week as opposed to a day. I gritted my teeth. Why draw the line at nailed-in deck boards when everything else was impossible to pull apart?

When the deck was assembled, they insisted on a staircase and railing. I told them no. I would take care of it. At that, I left for the day. They stayed and built both, citing liability concerns. With everything, and more, complete, the Illuminati provided a bill. It was the agreed price with no promised discount for my three weeks of labor. We'd been taken by the company from start to finish and had to pay for something not built the way we wished. The entire process proved to be a nightmare. But it was one of many for that spring.

Between helping to build the deck, we needed to finish prepping the old house for its future owner and our exit. A house sale and moving ... sounds pretty simple doesn't it? List the house, show it, sell it. Once it's sold, go and pack up, close, and hand the buyer the keys so that they can add to the house's legacy. It wasn't so simple with Stewart Little. The guy was an entitled toad who felt as though he could demand anything he wanted from anyone. But ...

We needed to sell the house as freedom was not going to simply drop into our laps. So it went on the day during my trip as I was trying to figure out where we were going to live ... if we were going to actually have to move and IF I was going to have a place to put my new motorcycle.

The appraisal came back and of course it was not high enough. If it had not been for all the deadbeat homeowners in our area who had been foreclosed on, it would have been fine. Unfortunately though, the appraiser was allowed to use those houses as comparable properties and, as such, they brought the value of our house down. If Mr. Little had been a decent guy, perhaps he would have made up the difference. Unfortunately the little toad gave us the ultimatum of accepting it or he would walk ... I was all set to tell him to simply kiss my ass and feel my foot up his. Our wonderful realtor settled me down and a deal was worked out between both realtors. So unfortunately the deal was still on.

Then came the "requirements." Everything had to be clean, all debris off the property, and all parts of the house had to be sterile. It had to be as built ... in 1790. My first thought in hearing this: Fuck you Stewart — for a $6000 deduction in sale price you can do it yourself. Unfortunately once again I was overruled. I spent the next three weeks moving and cleaning, cursing the whole time and imagining Stewart a little mouse, and all the ways a mouse can suffer and die. Broken neck anyone?

The final week eventually approached, we were cleaning everything and finding items we never thought we had, including some old chocolate. Since I am a person who loves chocolate I could not bear to toss it, but it did look suspect. Autumn dared me to eat it and so I did. Within a day I regretted that decision. I was as sick as I had ever been in my entire life. Autumn may have believed it was due to stress, but in reality it was severe food poisoning caused by VERY old moldy chocolate. Possibly death by chocolate had I been of lesser constitution.

With me now sick, we headed up to Canada for Autumn's eye appointment. Sure we were heading north when we were supposed to be headed to the closing. BUT had I been required to sit across from Stewart, I would not have sold the house and probably would have been taken out in handcuffs for assaulting him.

Especially when I learned that during a simple "walk-through" he decided to stay for HOURS just finding things to complain about. He complained about things that were NOT EVEN ON THE PROPERTY!!!! Unfortunately we were in Canada by that time and through the help of our realtor everything was taken care of before closing. It was best for all that I was leaving the country for the house had to get sold, and I could not do the things that I wanted to do to that man.

Good riddance to the little rat ...

—Adam

YURT CONSTRUCTION
JUNE 4, 5, & 6, 2010

"I've broken my femur. I think the idea of cave rafting is exciting and have begged my parents to let me learn to hang glide. PRK [eye surgery] was the most terrifying and painful thing I've ever done."

\- Autumn: 29 May 2010

"We've been homeless for nearly three weeks. Today the yurt arrives - via Fed Ex. I can't believe my new home is arriving on a box truck with a tracking number!"

\- Autumn: 4 June 2010

I'm a "take a quick peek and then look before you chicken-out" sort of girl. With my incredibly poor vision, contacts to my exact prescription were not available. I knew I wanted my vision corrected, but the most research I had done on my eye surgery was to find out that PRK was more invasive than Lasik, had a longer recovery time, a high success rate, and minimal amount of side effects. My terrible vision also gave me a high chance of regression. Meaning that in a few years, I may need to have a touch-up surgery performed. That was why I chose Canada.

My surgery came with not only a cheaper price tag than in the states at a highly professional and well reviewed medical facility, it also had a five-year guarantee. Any problems between day one and the end of five years would be fixed for free.

I woke up the morning of May 14th and did not even think about the sale of the house. I was too full of hopes and fears for what my day held. I did take a minute to realize, as I tried to mask how incredibly nervous I was, that I would never have seen our old house without glasses or contacts. I would never see the yurt with the need to wear such things. If all went well.

That day and the week that followed are a blur of a different sort. The surgery went well. It was horribly frightening. I declined a Valium because my low blood pressure meant that anything supposed to induce calm generally makes me fall asleep. I faced having both of my eyes frozen, my corneas scrubbed off, and a laser shot through my pupils with nothing more than a squeeze ball in my hand. I don't recommend that.

I expected fear and nervousness, pain and healing. What I didn't expect were the complications. With Lasik, you can pretty much see clearly when you leave the office. Healing is a few days. With PRK, I left the office with some pain pills and prescriptions. I walked back to the hotel with my eyes closed and my hand on Adam's arm. When I heard the sale had gone through, I nodded and rolled over to take more pain meds. I did not open my eyes.

That is how much of my week went. Sunlight, lamplight, just about any light was too much. If my eyes were open, they were watering. Adam kept mostly to the bathroom. His internal illness raged in full force. We functioned by eating takeout, using the fridge in the room, and trusting the dogs would take us to the park to do their business. When Adam was too sick, I walked the dogs alone squinting behind sunglasses.

Yet by the end of the week, the medical center was happy with my progress and waived the two-week checkup. I was free to go home until my six-month appointment. Adam drove. I recovered at his parents' house. We were officially homeless now. But home was on its way.

Convalescing as I was, I couldn't sit still. I bought a pair of dark safety glass that eclipsed my peripheral vision and headed outside. It wasn't enough. The sun pierced my eyes from the brilliant sky. The answer to that problem came in the form of a Tilley hat.

Looking like I was only missing a trench coat to mask my identity, I headed out into the May spring to alleviate the construction itch that was forming.

With some old scrap wood and the new power drill/screwdriver, I knocked together some raised beds for the garden. I was still wary of the idea of growing vegetables. The three years I had tried at the old house the bountiful harvest of weeds, poor amount of sunlight, and limited time to do anything about either problem led me to join a CSA. But now, Adam was hinting that a small raised garden would be fun. I had my doubts, but I did have time and power tools, along with a strong desire to build something. In the end, we tucked four raised beds along the low side of the deck and filled them with compost from a local dairy. I was in no rush to find plants.

We received the shipment notice on the yurt for June 1st. By the time the morning of June 4th rolled around, I had changed my plans from a half-day at work to taking the day off. It wasn't just that we were so excited to get our new home and start work on it. There were three other forces at play. The first was that I had to be at work on Monday for the beginning of a review for the offices I oversaw. The second was that the following four weekends Adam would be gone to a training course, so the weekend of June 5-6 was our one shot to get the yurt up. Lastly, it was scheduled to rain on Saturday and Sunday. Friday, June 4th was to be the only sunny day of the weekend.

We'd kept the yurt platform, a.k.a. our future floor, dry with a tarp since it had been finished in early May. Not that it had rained, or snowed, much during May. Now that it was June and our future home was due to arrive, the forecast called for day after day of rain. If we could just get the roof up, we would have a dry, or semi-dry, place to work underneath.

So anxious and excited, Adam and I waited through sunny hour after sunny hour. Fed Ex said our "package" was out for delivery. We were hoping that our delivery would be first on the truck, even middle would be okay. We paced the sun across the sky. As it touched the clouds forming to the west, we finally gave up hope. We'd seen this before in Maine. Rural deliveries via big carriers were sometimes sent back to the shipment center at the end of a long day to be rerouted the following day. Would Fed Ex ship on Saturday or were we out of luck until Monday? How would we build our home if it didn't come until the next week with our lack of available time?

Then my cell phone rang. It was the truck driver. He had our package at the end of the road and just wanted to check if he needed to pull in or back up the gravel road. It was 5 o'clock, the sun would still be shining for another three hours, and our new home had just arrived.

When Pacific Yurts had said our yurt would arrive via box truck, I had thought delivery truck. What pulled up the road was a massive 16-wheeler. The top of the cab hit the not-so-low branches on trees. Our seven bundles were the last items in the back. The driver took a long look at me, the Jeep, and trailer meant to receive the bundles and jumped in the back to give Adam a hand unloading. He wasn't supposed to, but a quick calculation on his part concluded that the fastest way home was to help.

Two bundles had some damage but nothing appeared broken. The worst result of the multi-state journey was rub marks on our French doors. The truck was unloaded in under twenty minutes and we were left with seven cartons of items, only a few of which I could pick up on my own. We signed the paperwork and the driver left us with packages scattered across the lawn and three hours of daylight. It was time to get to work.

We'd received the assembly instructions with the order confirmation and had been reading them for weeks. My hope was that they would make more sense when I had the materials in front of me. Otherwise we would be stuck by step three.

All materials were hauled over to the yurt platform. I carried over the polycarbonate dome, holding its five-foot expanse over my head in imitation of an alien spacecraft crossing the shadowy yard. The rafter bundle was so heavy and awkward that we had to cut it open and carry them in groups of four to six. Forty-two rafters later, we opened the instructions to page one. It was six o'clock on a spring evening in June.

The yurt would sit on a round platform four inches above the deck. Built with a lip that served as part of the anchor for the lattice walls, the first step was to cut a notch for the door. We had spent days with rudimentary measurements and tape laying out where we wanted the windows, the best view for the door, and prevailing wind angles. We had a good idea of where to begin. With a double check of measurements, Adam took the jigsaw to the platform. Our part of the construction had officially begun.

Organizing and spreading out the components to our new home

The next step consisted of standing the ten-foot high bundle of lattice upright and unrolling it around the platform edge. It took both Adam and I to position the massive thing, feeling like it would tip at any moment. We were over halfway around the platform, spreading and stretching the wall as we went, before the height dropped to eight feet and we felt like we had any control over the diminishing bundle. Unrolled around the perimeter, the lattice came to just under seven feet in height.

Something that had been mind boggling in the instructions, attaching the lattice to the door, made complete sense in person. With hardly an hour gone by, the lattice was up and secured to the front door, which we used for the first time. Before being secured to the platform, we checked to make sure the lattice was a uniform height over the entire expanse. It took some trial and error to efficiently tackle this step. Varieties of measuring sticks transitioned into a pole with a notch that Adam walked with next to the lattice while I kept an eye out for bumps or dips. Finally the lattice was secured to the base and we had what appeared to be a giant playpen with a French door.

Lattice wall in place as the shadows lengthen

Adam took charge for the next step, one that just did not make sense in my mind. An airline cable had to be run along the top of the lattice and then joined above the door. He wove it around the circle like he put up yurts daily while I shook my head.

Daylight was fading as we started moving rafters into the yurt and brought in the center ring. It was dark enough that I could finally take off my sunglasses. The next step, inserting one end of a rafter into the center ring and then hooking the other over the airline cable was problematic. It took a minimum of three rafters up to tenuously support the center ring. Rafters crashing down, bringing along the center support, was a possibility until at least eight were installed. Rafters falling out were a possibility until the screws attaching them to the cable were installed. The instructions said three to four people were needed for this part.

Adam had a plan. He had rented a drywall lift that reached twelve feet. The top of the yurt would be thirteen, but the starting rafters would only be able to raise the center ring a mere ten feet or so. We strapped the center ring to the lift and jacked it up to nine feet. I pulled a ladder over next to the lift and Adam picked up the first rafter.

With me inserting the rafter pins into the center ring and Adam forcing his end over the cable, the first four rafters were up in no time. The sun had set. In the fading dusk, we installed ten more rafters before admitting the darkness was getting the better of us. It was the realization that we needed to screw four brackets between rafters and the center ring as part of the high wind kit and neither of us could see the holes in the brackets that told us day one was over. We fell asleep hoping the forecasters would be wrong about the weekend's weather.

The first rafters connected to the center ring while being supported by a drywall lift and next to the 12' ladder

Adam woke me up to a gray morning. By the time we scarfed down a quick breakfast, a drizzling mist had moved in. Determined to carry on, we hunted for our hiking rain gear to realize it had been packed, and never unpacked, during the final days of the move. The only rain gear we could find belonged to our motorcycle equipment. Adam donned Frog Togs and I put on a stylish red and and black one-piece First Gear rainsuit that was too big. Rolled up cuffs and hems were not going to improve the water resistance, but it was the best we could do.

I did find one immediate advantage to the overcast weather. I could see. The massive, light filtering wrap-around safety glasses were tossed aside. Better, the constant moisture soothed my healing corneas. I felt almost normal for the first time since PRK.

With the rain, our Jeep Wrangler became a mobile tool shed. We dispensed with installing the wind kit brackets that had ended our construction the night before with the new drill tucked in a ziplock bag. Happily the next step of the day required no tools other than a ladder, the drywall lift, and brute force. We still had 28 rafters to install. With each additional rafter, the center ring rose higher. We raised the drywall lift and eventually unstrapped the center ring. The lift was moved away and the nearly complete roof rose over us.

As we moved around to install the last rafters spaced evenly across the roof, I was at the top of the 12-foot ladder. The tension on the airline cable was so great that Adam had to jam his shoulder into the lattice to push it out in order to hook the rafter onto the cable. The result was that the displaced lattice would loosen the tension on neighboring rafters.

A rafter crashed. The noise alone made both of us jump, me nearly off the ladder. It also hit Adam's foot. I shimmied down the ladder to make sure he was okay. After a brief spite of hopping around followed by a discussion of tactics, I put a hard hat on his head and climbed back up to my perch. I soon found myself balancing on the edge of the ladder, trying to hold the end of the one rafter being installed while supporting three to four adjacent rafters with shoulder/forearm/hand/anything available. It was yoga at a 12-foot elevation on a four-inch by ten-inch platform in the rain.

Three more rafters fell, none as close to hitting Adam as the first. Our rate of assembly was faster than the raining rafters and we continued to make progress. Until the first thunderstorm moved in. It took a few rumbles before I realized I was standing on a 12-foot metal ladder next to a metal drywall lift. I suddenly decided it was time for a tea break and down I went until the storm rolled over.

Despite the weather and falling structural elements, we had all the rafters installed before lunch. With quick functionality, Adam zipped around the outside of the yurt installing a screw to trap each rafter onto the metal cable. Now, they would stay in place. To help us celebrate, the sun came out. Which meant the rain gear came off and I put on my sunglasses. We were on to step two for the day: rafter supports.

As part of the snow load kit, each rafter had come with a 2x4 that would help channel extra weight from the roof. Each of the 42 eight-foot long 2x4s had one side cut at an angle to match the slope of the roof. The height of the lattice walls was just under seven feet. Every yurt assembly is a unique process dependent on exact platform size, construction, and attention to details. So the rafter supports were left long to be cut to fit perfectly. We took some random measurements of floor to rafter height to determine length, gratefully pulled the chop saw onto the rain free deck, and started cutting.

Forty-two chops later, we started the pre-drilling process. Each rafter support would be attached to a rafter via two metal plates at the top and to the floor with two metal brackets at the base. Each piece required four screws. We shredded the first template within ten rafters due to the lingering damp. After a quick laminating process with packing tape, the process became a smooth tandem operation. First Adam would pre-drill the eight holes on the beam and then I would attach the four metal brackets. When we got tired, we switched. It took hours.

When all 42 supports were ready, we then wedged them under each rafter, pre-drilled the holes into the rafters, and screwed the supports in place. We quickly abandoned pre-drilling into the floor as a time waster. As Adam finished attaching the last of the top brackets to the rafter, something he could far more easily do at his six-foot-plus height, I began pre-drilling through the lattice.

Each support also had to be screwed into the lattice wall in two places from the outside. It was for this reason we hadn't simply skipped this step to be accomplished after the walls and roof coverings were in place. Once the coverings were up, there would have been no way to access the outside of the lattice wall. We had deemed the perimeter blocking, a custom cut board that ran from rafter support to adjacent rafter support, was something that could wait. It could at least be finished when the coverings were in place.

The sun had set by the time the last rafter support was fully secured. It had been a very long and slow day. Although the accomplishments seemed small, in reality we had come a long way. The entire structure, looking like a bare bones eclectic garden arbor, was more solid than our recently sold 200-year-old house. The finished framework stood airy and graceful in the fading light. It was the fact that the framework was complete that sent us to bed smiling. In the morning, we would start the final phase. We could finally cover our new home.

**The yurt frame with rafter supports going in during one of the
few sunny moments late in the afternoon of day 2**

We woke to torrential showers. No mere drizzling mist, but
deluges. I gave a wry thought to our weeks of trying to keep the
platform dry. Why bother? Our new home made a great wading
pool. Over breakfast we studiously reviewed the weather radar.
Rain from edge to edge on the screen, but there were lighter bands
within the downpours. If we could get the roof up during one of
those, we would have a chance to finish.

Our first chance came mid-morning and we were ready for it.
Wearing motorcycle rain gear for the second day, we headed out as
the downpour slowed. We hauled the three bundles for the roof
covering over to the yurt and opened the one for the liner. A cream
color, the liner was a flimsy covering designed to hide the silver
insulation that would go on second. The last piece was the taupe
colored roof. Both the liner and the roof material were polyvinyl.
The insulation was a NASA designed bubble wrap between two
sheets of aluminum foil. At least that is all it looked like. We were
hoping the reviews that said it really did work to keep the yurt
warm in the winter would prove to be true. But that was a worry
for another day. Today, we were just happy nothing was cotton and
likely to get moldy if soaked. Because everything was going to get
doused before the day was out. We were already dealing with drips
running down our sleeves every time we lifted something.

The liner didn't even weigh one pound and was a cinch to take up the ladder to then unfold, shake, and toss in order to spread it out. My only fear was that we would unfold it inside out so that the seams showed. Luckily, we got it right the first try. Tiny puffs of wind toyed with the newly situated edge as I took up the insulation.

Being bulky, the insulation came in a large origami bundle of folds. Unlike the other two roof components, you did not spread it out halfway and then pull one layer over the center of the roof to unfold into one seamless piece. The insulation was seamed. And the seam needed to be taped.

Under fitful bursts of rain, Adam and I unfolded the insulation first one way and then the other. A silver cover spread across our yurt roof until we met in the back. I took up the foil tape and started it going from the center dome opening, but I could only get it to run five feet down. The yurt diameter was 24 feet, so we had a good 12 feet on a slant that the tape needed to go. I began to wonder if some of the instructions weren't designed as a joke to see if anyone would really follow through with every step.

Despite his fear of heights Adam braved the high center ladder, taking with him a long stick. He managed to force the roll down the seam to within six feet of the edge. At that point I could hook it from an eight-foot ladder on the ground outside the yurt and unroll it the remaining bit. We slapped the tape down as best we could and got ready for the last step.

The instructions for the top cover called for two to three strong people to carry the unwieldy bundle up a scaffold through the center of the roof where I'd been stationed. That opening is where the five-foot round skylight/vent would be placed. While building the yurt it was ground zero for every roof related activity. Now with just Adam and I, we gazed skyward at the thirteen feet separating the top cover from its destination.

Adam's idea was to use the drywall lift to get the top cover up twelve feet and then manhandle the bundle the last foot through the center ring. The first problem was that I couldn't lift half the top cover from the floor up the four feet to the top of the drywall lift. We almost made it once, but it slid off the 'H' shaped frame. We tossed a piece of plywood on the drywall lift and tried again.

Now with an added obstacle that didn't stay put, I just couldn't get my side up high enough. Adam's dad came to give us a hand. Our window of light rain was coming to an end. The wind was starting to pick up, lifting the edge of the insulation as rain pelted on our half-finished roof. Stressed, Adam and his dad gave the awkward bundle a mighty heave. Halfway to the lift, Adam dropped his side and fell to the sodden floor moaning in pain.

Adam is young and in good shape. But ever since an accident when he was twelve, he has had a vertebrate that would slip out of alignment and drop him if he turned the wrong way. In the ten years I'd known him, his disk had slipped only three or four times. But I had never seen him go down so hard or fast. He lay in the inch of water on the floor gasping for air, struggling with a pain he described as having a chef's knife stabbing through his chest to his spine. And boy was he pissed.

Breezes were turning into gusts and rain was coming down hard. If we didn't want to lose everything we'd done that morning to the wind, we had to keep going. With no one else to fall back on, Adam's dad helped me lift the top cover onto the drywall lift. Somehow, we got it precariously positioned. He began to hoist the lift upwards while I climbed the ladder keeping one hand on the cover to steady it. If it fell off, I just wanted to make sure that it didn't land on top of anyone.

At the wobbly 12-foot full extension of the lift, I faced the sliding weight of the top cover alone. Adam's eyes were riveted on me from where he lay below still unable to get up. Somehow, I managed to get one edge of the awkward bundle onto the top ring. I struggled, cursed, and managed to pull up almost half of the cover. And that was it. I just couldn't get the remainder up onto the roof. The cover remained suspended one bump or gust away from hurtling back to the floor and hopefully not ripping or taking out something on the way down.

The insulation was lifting nearly halfway across the dome with each gust. With no options left, I swapped with Adam's dad and watched someone else take over while I watched from the floor. I expected the cover to drop with every step his dad took up the ladder, but it held. With one massive shove, he managed to force the cover off the lift and onto the center ring and rafters.

I spun the lift out of the way and dashed outside to shout instructions through the storm on what to do next. Unlike Adam and I, his dad hadn't been prepping for yurt construction for three weeks. The trickiest part was finding the notch that fit over the front door. As I fumbled through the reams of the top cover looking for the one section I needed in order to ensure the entire cover would be unfolded properly, a strong rain-filled gust struck the yurt. The insulation jumped a foot in the air. Adam was the only one who didn't have his hands full. Pain or no, he leapt up and grabbed the insulation before it flipped over and had to be repositioned. The action snapped his vertebrae back in line, but he remained sweating with pain as he held on to the insulation and yurt wall.

Finally, I found the door notch in the top cover. Adam's dad and I began the process of unfolding the top cover with me on an eight-foot ladder outside the yurt and him at the center dome. Once it was half unfolded, Adam tied sturdy ropes to the grommet holes. We walked them to the far side of the yurt and together pulled half the cover up and over. With that act, the yurt was finally covered. The heavy polyvinyl of the final layer did not even buffet in the gusting rain.

We stood under it a moment. For the first time, I heard the drumming of rain against my new roof. We were both soaked. Adam kept having spasms of pain. We were emotionally overwhelmed. With the new band of heavy rain flooding in, we took a break. I hunted for my bag from Canada and found the last of my super pain meds to give to Adam. We had 40 minutes until the heaviest rain swept through. We spent it in a daze, drinking tea and coffee and eating granola bars.

When we could get back out, we switched out the order of installation. The last step was supposed to be the acrylic top dome that covered the center ring. With light rain still falling, we wanted to finish weatherizing the roof. I climbed the ladder to install a beam across the top ring where our yet to be purchased fan would someday hang. Adam tied ropes to the top dome.

The five-foot dome was larger than the center ring as it was designed to fit over it. Therefore, it had to be installed from the outside. The only way to get it in place was to slide it along the outside on the newly covered roof. We placed the bag that the top cover had come in under it lest we somehow rip our new roof. Adam hauled it into place and flipped it over the opening. Then came the tricky part.

No matter how many times I had read the instructions, I could never fully follow how to install the top dome. There were four attachment points. One was a semi-hinge, two tensioners, and one strange assembly that allowed the dome to lift a few inches in order to vent the yurt. I read a few bits of what seemed to be complicated instructions aloud to Adam. He leaned over the ladder as I showed him an illustration of what had to go where. "Oh, is that it?" He turned back to the task at hand and had the dome installed in under five minutes. Finally, no more rain fell from above. Just from the sides.

The newly installed center dome weathering its first storm

We turned our attention to the final part of the yurt puzzle: the sidewalls. We spread out the wall panels in the relative safety under the roof. The insulated panels already had the cream colored liner attached and were numbered. All we had to do was hang each one from the top cover using 'S' hooks until everything was situated. Working clockwise, we put up the six blank panels and five window panels in no time.

Even with the relatively easy assembly at this point, we were nearly done in. We walked back to his parents' house watching the silver insulation of the walls dance in the fitful wind of the rainstorm under the cream colored dome. The entire assembly at this point looked like a strange alien spacecraft, or at least like we were trying to hide one. We were giddy. The worst was over but we were cold and tired. Still the finish was in sight and would lure us back out into the rainy day after another quick break to warm up.

Despite the action packed morning, it was only 11 o'clock when we headed out to install the deep, forest green side cover. It came in a rolled tube of polyvinyl that you unrolled counter-clockwise, opposite the installation of the insulation panels. Every few feet, we had to twist click a plastic lock onto a cord that came attached to the roof cover valance. Around the yurt perimeter we went. In under twenty minutes we were straightening the insulation to match the windows and snapping the final clips in place.

The rain had let up to a light mist. But everything had gone through a good dousing and as we finished clipping in the side covers, sheets of water from the roof fell on us as we flipped the valance down. So close to being finished, we persevered. The final attachment for the walls was to the French door.

The custom made door had side clamps hidden behind fascias. The extra side cover needed to be wrapped around a wooden bar that ran the length of the door. The bar and cover then had to be wedged into the clamps on the door. All of this had to be done from the inside through the lattice framework. I stayed outside smoothing the yurt cover and trying to help wedge the wooden bar into the clamps. Adam tackled the intricacies of the operation from the inside. It took several tries on each side but eventually the sidewall was clamped into the door and the fascia boards were replaced.

We now had a covered yurt. All that was left was to attach the sidewalls to the platform with a screw located every foot around the perimeter. There were over 70 screws. I'd taken off my rainsuit due to its oversized bulk. Between the light rain and everything being wet, my jeans were soaked through. The wind gave me a chill while my core body temperature dropped. Low blood sugar started to drive the downward spiral faster. It was after noon and despite the recent break, I gave up. I walked back to Adam's parents' house and straight into the shower. I didn't come out until I was warm again.

After some hot food, I was no longer shaking and ready to continue. I helped Adam, who'd followed me inside, by pulling down the side cover while he screwed it in place.

The newly installed door! The sheen on the floor is water.

The gray sky was bright when we stood up from the last screw. It was only 3 o'clock on Sunday. The yurt was fully assembled. It had taken us less than 48 hours even with the rain.

—Autumn

"I don't care what they say, they don't have them like this in Mongolia!!"

- Adam: 4 June 2010

utumn's PRK proved a bit fun for me as well as her. Not only was I suffering from food poisoning (at least the laser center had a wonderful bathroom!), the laser procedure was unnerving. I knew what it entailed, but sitting in the waiting room listening to the equipment zap my wife's eyes was very disturbing! I tried to block the worst ideas of what was going on in the next room from my mind. At least she didn't scream.

Autumn came out in a daze with a prescription for pain meds. Since it was her prescription, she had to get it filled. Moncton, New Brunswick at the time was rather rough. I imagined that many of the local transients were aware there were many easy targets who were blind, or half-blind, carrying some pretty nice pain meds. Needless to say I was on edge as we walked from the pharmacy to the hotel with a rather obvious Lasik MD bag in Autumn's hand. But fortunately with the exception of one very angry vagrant who may have gotten seriously hurt had he attacked us, given my very protective nature of my then-helpless wife, we managed to make it back to the hotel.

The week was spent making sure Autumn was properly attended to the best I could and it passed fairly well even if she was more blind than sighted and I needed a bathroom every 15 minutes. We eventually arrived back in Maine to await the yurt. For three weeks we waited patiently for our home to arrive, staying in a room at my parents' house. Every day we checked the tracking number and watched as our new home travelled closer. It could not have come soon enough as our time spent with my parents was very tense. Autumn and I were accustomed to a whole house and our ways, which didn't mesh well with staying under my parents' roof. When the yurt arrived, it would be a relief to finally be on our own again.

The yurt construction was as intense as Autumn described it. A combination of reading the directions and overcoming obstacles, we constructed it in rainstorms as templates shredded, the instructions doused, and power tools kept dry in plastic bags. For two days we were soaked, as well as our new home, making me wonder why I'd tried so hard to keep the yurt platform dry. During the initial construction, the yurt door was positioned about 195 degrees S by SW to allow for winter sun, as well as privacy from the neighbors. It was an idea that resulted in good and bad ramifications.

Autumn reading the instruction book during day 1

The biggest challenge was the weather. My great grandmother once called our New England spring storms the "May Storm" as summer did not start until it came through. Unfortunately, the storm decided to come the day after the yurt arrived. Given the amount of work the drills we'd used to build the yurt went through, I cannot begrudge the quality of Mikita brand LXT series we used through the whole ordeal! Autumn had initially questioned the expense of new power tools, but having two battery powered drivers helped the process immensely. But after watching the deck construction, I knew we needed them as our outdated equipment would never survive the heavy use. Autumn agreed by the end of day one that they were a great idea.

To assemble a yurt, it is best to have a team and good weather. A couple can do it, but a team can do it better. The weather ... not much can be done about a streak of bad luck!

— Adam

The completed yurt

MOVING IN
JUNE 7 - 30, 2010

"When no one is looking, I can levitate things. And if I hum and clap my hands, all the furniture in the shed rearranges itself. At least that is my story on how I got the furniture from the shed to the yurt."

- Autumn: 13 June 2010

I came home from work and Adam was looking bashful. It was the Wednesday following yurt construction. My head was still spinning with the office review, which was going well even if I had to present to the reviewers wearing sunglasses and my Tilley hat while inside. I took off the hat during my PowerPoint presentation. I kept on the sunglasses.

At first I thought his shy smile had something to do with the yurt. He'd been hoping to paint the floor this week. Sunday afternoon and Monday he had swept out the standing water puddled on our new floor. We'd made a decision to skip the debate about flooring types, hardwood versus bamboo or maybe pergo, and gone straight to 'slap some paint on it and decide later.' With all the windows open and the top dome vented, we were just waiting for it to dry out.

Then I spied the garden. The four raised beds I'd built and we'd filled with compost with the understanding that there was no real need to buy plants this year, after all we had a lot going on, were dotted with leafy green seedlings.

Our tiny garden!

"What the?"

Adam launched into an introduction of the types and varieties of seedlings now spaced through our garden patch.

"These are heirloom varieties of tomatoes," he said to justify his seedling shopping spree. "And six lettuce seedlings too. That way they'll be ready to eat sooner. You always take salad in your lunch in the summer."

He'd won me over to living in a yurt. Agreeing to raise a garden of seedlings was not a difficult case for him to sell. The three plants of zucchini had me worried, but I was in love by the time we got to the herb patch.

"You mean you bought celery but not basil? And hot peppers but no green? We have to go back."

So began our first summer gardening in three years. We hadn't even moved into our new home, but that was on the agenda. The floor finally dried enough for the first coat of paint. Adam and I hooked a utility trailer to the back of the jeep and went to visit the shed.

There were a lot of things we would need to make living in the yurt possible. The kitchen table, something to cook on, and chairs topped the list. But for now all we wanted was one thing: our futon. It was still too damp to seriously consider sleeping in the yurt yet. But I was hoping for a first night before Adam disappeared to his training for the weekend on Friday night.

Before heading to his parents' house and our borrowed bedroom, he showed me the other accomplishment for the day. We had bought two awning kits for the yurt windows. Even though there were five windows plus the French doors, only two had a strong southern exposure and no trees. Adam had tackled putting together the complicated frame of poles, figured out how to weave the zip closure for the acetate window through the frame, and fasten the construction with the snaps that usually help to hold the window covering closed.

We spent our first night in the yurt that Thursday, June 10th. With no sink, bathroom, cooking equipment or clothes, the yurt functioned like a nighttime retreat. We needed to shower at the in-laws' and walk back in the morning for breakfast and work clothes. But it was worth it.

For the first time we heard the wind caress the fabric walls. The interior with the exposed red pine rafters and lattice against the cream liner was mentally soothing. There is something sacred and safe about a round space. I would not have believed it before, but now I was drawn to my circular home in a way I couldn't explain. I felt content there. I wanted to sit under the vaulted rafters bathed in light and not worry about work or money or what was for dinner. The yurt inspired quiet and peace. It was a wonderful first night.

Window awning installed

When I got home Friday night, I had an agenda. Adam was gone until late Sunday. For the weekend, I planned to begin building a small room directly below the yurt. This space would function as storage for our small home and, critically, a place to keep the battery bank belonging to our future solar panel. But for Friday's goal, I simply wanted to get some furniture in the yurt so it would be livable.

Adam and I have a few traits in common, the strongest of which is a dislike of having to ask for help. I hitched up the trailer to the Jeep and parked the combo in front of the shed as soon as I got home from work. I assured my in-laws that I might put in a few items that night and would let them know on Saturday what I needed help with.

Happily, my in-laws go to sleep early. In the summer, that translates to 'still daylight.' As soon as all was quiet, I was raiding the shed. With no one to watch me in fear, or with words of common sense, I scaled bins and bureaus in search of a select list of items. I wanted the two dressers from the bedroom, the oak table and chairs, the coffee table, and an antique icebox. One thing I dearly wanted but would not risk moving on my own was a massive oak shrunk. The top of this wall sized piece of furniture had leaded glass cabinet doors while the bottom portion's dimensions were over two and one-half feet by four feet. Assembled, this one piece of furniture would function as my kitchen center from silverware to plates to ingredient storage until something else could be built. It would just fit beneath the rafters where they met the yurt wall at seven feet high. To move that, I was going to wait for Adam.

We'd stored the last hectically stuffed pieces of furniture in no particular order. There were items we wanted to sell mixed with pieces I needed to find. The antique oak icebox was lined with zinc and weighed nearly 100 pounds. It was against the back wall directly across from the door. I kept my eye on it as I rearranged bureaus, hauled out the table, found and removed the dressers. When I'd found and put everything else I was looking for on the trailer, there was a two-foot wide corridor from the door to the icebox. I had to try.

The boxes on top of the icebox were shoved up and over to a set of bins. The handlebars to a bicycle jutted into my way and required turning them and the icebox first one way and then the other. Inch by inch I waddled the icebox from storage and to the edge of the shed. When I reached bare ground, I realized I had a problem.

I'd been walking the icebox across the hard floor. It was far beyond my strength to pick up and carry. I could only lift a corner an inch through counterbalancing. On the soft, uneven ground between the shed and the trailer, it wouldn't budge. Looking around, I located a board. It took half an hour to 'walk' the icebox the six feet from shed to trailer. I was very content when I did. Strapping everything down, I merrily drove my haul back to the yurt at dusk.

The nice thing about unloading is that everything simply had to come off. There was no rearranging of a stocked shed full of items that compared to a game of advanced Tetris to move one bureau. I'd discovered that the old oak table was cartable by turning it sideways and holding onto the tree sized support. The dressers were not a challenge with the drawers removed. Except I wanted to stack them. Mine was smaller and heavier. It took a few tries and a daunting lift to finally hoist my dresser on top of Adam's and slide it to stability. I gave his a scratch in the process, but they looked fantastic, like one solid unit, when finally re-drawered. That left the icebox.

With fading light hiding the struggle, I used a board once again to maneuver the benignly sized block of wood and metal. It was the three steps up to the deck that really had me worried. The icebox proved amazingly solid as it withstood rocking, sliding on its back against an upper step, crazy leans, and a final shove. No antique should be put through such a test. I was immensely proud as I settled it into the yurt in its new home near the door. I called it a successful night, took a shower and went to bed.

It took my in-laws a little while to realize what I'd pulled off, which only happened when I came by the house to move out my box of clothes. I was given a quick lecture which involved the stacked dressers as an example of something too big and heavy for me to move on my own. I nodded and did not point out that the icebox had been far worse. The dressers I could pick up on my own at least.

Through an odd fate, Adam and I had matching his and her dressers before we met!

At that point I decided to fall back on a story I'd once used to explain a large boulder that I'd moved up a hill to use as part of an ornamental cairn in a garden at the old house.

"I can levitate things when no one is watching."

The brilliant thing about this argument is that though no one believes it, there is no way to disprove it. I added a new variation as everyone in the family knew the shed had been an organization nightmare.

"When I hum and clap my hands, the shed rearranges itself."

There was no need to try to prove that. I was done in the shed and busy now with building walls for the storage room beneath the yurt. Framing between deck posts, one side of which had 45-degree supports to the decking to work around, on ground that pitched catty-cornered to the room was easy after the icebox episode. Between unpacking clothes and setting up a camp kitchen on a workbench Adam had brought from the old garage, I had two walls built by the time Adam came home Sunday afternoon.

Framing in the under yurt storage area

He took one look at the relocated furniture and then turned to me. I grinned.

"I need your help getting the shrunk."

"Really? If you can levitate things you should have been able to move it up here on your own."

He can always figure out a good challenge to my logic. "It has glass. I was afraid someone would look out the window, see me, and it'd fall and break."

Adam laughed. We went and got the shrunk.

The yurt began to take on the disparate qualities of having the comforts of home, including massive pieces of oak furniture, and still feel like we were camping out for the summer. My dishes and glassware were on display tucked into the top of the shrunk, silverware handily placed in one of the two drawers. Our dressers held summer clothes and we breakfasted at our old table. Yet the cooking area consisted of a recycled work table, a single burner butane camp stove, and running water from a five-gallon Coleman water container.

The oak table and German shrunk

Our fridge was an antique icebox. This family heirloom was one where you put blocks of ice in the top which would cool the food stored in the chamber below. Melted water dripped down a long pipe to a tray placed under the icebox which was hidden by an oak 'flap.' Ice needed to be changed every two days and the water emptied twice. The storage was just over two cubic feet.

Claiming independence, we used a solar shower instead of Adam's parents'. Almost as soon as I was home from work, I would put on a bikini and take my shower. The tepid water rested on the highest corner of the deck while I stood on a small platform beneath. It was functional and often brisk.

One place where there was no doubt we were not on our own was electricity. An umbilical extension cord snaked through the lawn from the main house to our yurt outpost. We had goals of installing a solar panel. We also had a budget. The yurt loan didn't have to begin to be repaid until August or so. I was hoping to use what would have gone toward the old mortgage to buy the solar equipment, batteries, and wood for further projects like a real kitchen and bathroom in the yurt. For the time being, we were only moderately independent.

It didn't stop us from bringing over the flat screen TV and setting it up on the coffee table. We watched DVDs while sitting in our massive tent. I felt akin to a nomad, but with heavier furniture.

So many things were in flux that nothing felt odd or permanent. Yes, I was using ice for keeping my groceries cool, but it worked. When something didn't work, we looked for alternatives. A propane fridge was only $100 for a cheap one, but reviews didn't make them sound like the best option. A solar powered fridge/freezer cost over $1000 and were out of the question until we bought some other basics. So I switched to buying Parmalait milk so that it didn't need to be refrigerated until open. The small square box took up less room, a huge boon, and was gone in three days, minimizing chance of spoilage from neglected ice on a hot day. The yurt ever so slowly was changing us.

The original makeshift, but well used, kitchen

Throughout June my weekend construction spree continued in Adam's absence. The remaining walls went up in the storage room. Soon we would have a home for the planned battery bank. With a bit of additional lumber, I built an outhouse. This was a strategic move to get us freed from the in-laws' bathroom until we could afford a composting toilet and I had a chance to build a private place for it in the yurt. After trudging across the lawn in all weather, a quick jaunt through the woods to a private room to take care of business was incredibly appealing.

The outhouse design was the beginning of a self realization process for me. We'd used some great outhouses while camping and some not so great. I wanted our temporary one to be pleasant. Initial ideas were complicated such as a mini-yurt based on a gazebo plan. But as I measured wood and time and became frustrated, I asked myself what I was doing. I just needed something that worked, not an architectural wonder. I scrapped pages of drawings and searched online. The Virginia Extension website offered several typical designs all the way down to pit depth. All made great use of the fact that plywood came in four-foot by eight-foot sheets. With some tiny tweaking, including the addition of two antique windows salvaged from the old house, I got to work. And I began to learn that complicated was not better. Functionally simple was a great achievement in and of itself.

By the end of June, the storage shed was complete as was the outhouse. Pre-painted plywood siding that Adam had bought for covering the storage had been carefully measured before cutting. I managed to make four sheets of plywood cover the four walls of the storage and three of the outhouse. I found an abandoned door from my in-laws' scrap pile for the fourth.

The judicious use of materials which managed to complete two projects with the materials for one had Adam scratching his head when he returned from his final weekend away. I explained it was due to a complicated set of numerological equations that only functioned near a full moon and allowed wood to be thinned just slightly to extend its mass. I don't think he bought it.

Adam was to be home full time now. The storage area was done. We had figured out how to cook and shower in our new nomadic home. Some boxes had been unpacked to locate essential kitchen items like dishes, pots, pans, and silverware. Clothes were put away. We now had a bathroom, the outhouse, which we dubbed "Wood's Hole" in a cheeky honor of the area of the world where Adam and I had met.

The completed under yurt storage room

It still felt very new to be in the yurt, like it was temporary even while it was comfortable. At some point we would have to solve the problem of supplying electricity, a better cooking area, and tackle the 80+ bins stored in the shed. Not to mention finding something to do with the furniture we didn't have room for in our 500-square-foot abode. We still had a lot to go though and it'd only just officially become summer.

— Autumn

"Really? You moved all this stuff by yourself ... sigh"
- Adam: 10 June 2010

I love gardening, to see the young little plants grow and flourish into tall and healthy adults, providing tasty and nutritious products for us to enjoy. It's a pleasure I have enjoyed since I was a toddler eating peas in the fenced-in garden that served as a play area. The idea of having a garden again was quite delightful and, of course, it had to be one of the first things I did to the yurt.

The second thing was painting the floor. I had a training for the next month and getting the floor finished was quite important as it needed to be done before anything could be moved into the yurt. I also was hoping Autumn would get a few "SMALL" things over to the yurt to make it a bit more livable and also expedite our departure from my parents' place.

Needless to say, upon arriving back from my first weekend away I found my lovely wife had somehow moved not only the dressers, the table, the bureaus, but also the antique fridge. So much for a small movement of items from our shed ... I could not complain though. The transfer made life easier and the one thing that I will never accuse her of is being dependent on someone to get something done. If it needs to be accomplished, she can do it and such an attribute is necessary when venturing into such a crazy adventure.

Independence is a valuable attribute for anyone. Having to rely on someone else can lead to disappointment and frustration. Given the tension at my parents' house it was paramount to cut the cord and support network completely.

There was an issue with the yurt construction and moving in of furniture that Autumn didn't mention. With each pound of weight that was added to the deck, it became more unstable. It swayed with every movement. In their rush to finish the project, the Illuminati failed to properly brace the deck. A call was made and Him of the Illuminati showed up very annoyed with a box of screws and some 2x4s. He promptly screwed them together and created 'X' braces to secure between supports. These minimized the sway but did not eliminate it.

By this point we were worn out. I was done dealing with these damn locals. I ended up installing more bracing and even redoing some of the Illuminati's mess. Then I fixed both the railings and the stairs. With the under-deck room Autumn built, the yurt felt mostly stable in all but the highest of north winds, which would cause the entire deck and yurt to harmonically vibrate. They hadn't used any metal hangers or brackets, just nails – vertical nails. Autumn was pretty sure that without the weight of the yurt the decking would lift if the right gust caught it.

The lessons learned in this deck experience was to never hire local contractors with no experience other than a sign on their truck door. Pay them only a daily rate, with a maximum limit, and NEVER for the entire job. Get multiple estimates, even if it means going far and wide. Finally and most importantly, if you have the time and inclination, do it yourself. The experience is valuable. Had we done this, the deck would have only cost us $2,400. Plus it would have been the way we wanted it. In the end we ended up paying $9000 for a shaky deck that would require a chainsaw and a wrecking crew to remove. Don't make the same mistake.

Wood's Hole

The best thing though was Wood's Hole. Don't judge, but I love using outhouses. Sure they smell occasionally, and there's a multitude of insects … but the idea of doing your business in nature is liberating. You are not confined by four walls and sanitized wet wipes. You are free to go freely – a wonderful experience!

Outhouses are a funny topic. Technically they are legal in Maine but in our case we simply overlooked the legal way of installing them and just put it up. It was on a hill in the forest. The door closed all right, but the privacy precluded the use more often than not. There were many times in the evening I would sit there, doing my business and see toads in the forest, the reflection of spiders' eyes in the leaves, and the movement of insects in the soil. I really became connected, adding my own biome to the forest ecosystem at the same time. ;)

— Adam

LET THERE BE LIGHT
JULY 2010

"Nothing ever goes according to schedule or budget."
- Autumn: 6 July 2010

"I have not lived so much outside since ... I don't remember. I have not had such a tan, been in such good shape, had so much energy ... just felt so healthy and really happy in years."
- Autumn: 17 August 2010

We scheduled the acquisition of improvements such as the solar panel, batteries, a ceiling fan, wood stove, chimney kit and such over the course of the summer. We didn't want to use the credit card. Our goal was to stay out of debt, pay off the yurt loan, and save some money so that we wouldn't be tied to 40-hour-a-week jobs. It sounded like a great plan as we created the strategy in the days before the yurt arrived.

We used the "shore" power from Adam's parents as sparingly as possible. The days were approaching the longest time of light, so we rarely needed extra illumination. To compensate for the few times when a night light was needed, Adam found LED lights at the grocery store for only $10. They worked off three AAA batteries and had two brightness levels. Coming in packs of three and with pivoting heads, we attached them to rafters around the yurt, including over my kitchen area. The light pretty much covered every area.

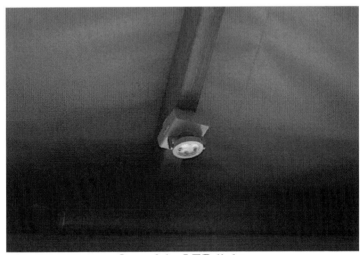

One of the LED lights

Beyond the lights, now that we were living in the yurt, we found things were not going as smoothly as visualized. Summer had just begun and already the yurt heated up quickly during the day. A fan to help vent the warm air would be a huge help. However, we didn't want to install a ceiling fan and run it off Adam's parents' electricity through the extension cord. It was time to cut ourselves loose.

Financially, we didn't have all we needed to buy the solar panel and batteries, plus the fan. Once we figured out the added cost for proper wires, connecters, and regulators the price was more than we'd figured by half again. But the need to make our new home livable finally overwhelmed our desire not to use the credit card. I gave Adam the green light for an equip-the-yurt shopping spree.

From the early yurt planning days, Adam had been in touch with a local green energy store. Now that it was time to get the parts we'd been discussing for two months, everything came together quickly. The order was placed in mid-June, Adam located and bought the wire needed to run from the solar panel to the batteries. At least, he bought what the majority of places recommended.

It seemed everyone had their own take on how to install solar. There was no one "buy this for this size house" plan that you could just purchase pre-packaged and off the shelf. Most helpful books appeared to have been written in the late 60s with a mid-80s update. Even our local store gave us theories without specifics. When it came down to it, no one was sure how much energy we'd need nor how much we'd store and use with one solar panel and batteries. Even the gauge of wires to run between batteries varied.

With the fact that we needed AC power in the yurt for the lights and kitchen supplies from the old house but were considering keeping the fan DC to run straight off the batteries, our heads were swimming. Well mostly Adam's. I'd taken the approach of "I just want to plug it in and make it work." I took inventory of the needed voltage of any major electrical appliance so that Adam could determine what size inverter we would need. In the end he made the executive decision and told me the bad news.

My beloved Dyson vacuum required far too much start-up power to be economically feasible to run on the one solar panel and four batteries he'd decided to go with. The cost of the inverter needed to handle the load was more than triple one that could handle everything else. I wanted to pout but it was fairly obvious that we couldn't buy the mega-inverter just so I could plug in a vacuum that would suck the batteries dry in a matter of minutes. We'd be left to recharge over days with little energy to spare so I could use a vacuum cleaner. Adam softened the blow by suggesting we could keep the extension cord for now, just so I could still use my virtually new vacuum. I agreed.

It was truly Christmas in July for Adam. As box after box arrived, he ripped into them and began sorting components. By the first Friday of July, he had assembled and set up the fan, installed the batteries, wired up the solar panel, and put in a wifi router. The only thing missing was a frame for the valuable solar panel.

When we'd had posts sunk to support the deck, we'd had one extra installed to support the future solar panel. But now we found out the support frame we'd liked was back ordered. All options were pricey. With just one panel, we needed to be able to change the angle it sat between winter and summer to capture the most light. Though we had a great exposure throughout the day, we thought the pole mount would give us options to change the solar alignment in the winter when the sun would be much lower.

Frustrated and overspent, we put the new panel flat on the corner of the deck. Adam plugged it in. Over a celebratory meal of coconut shrimp, fried bananas, and a salad, we sat outside in the sun knowing that its bright light was powering more than optimism. Everything seemed to work on the first try and surprisingly, the solar panel on the deck sucked in a huge amount of light. The worst problem came from shadows cast by the railing as well as inducing dire fears of stepping on it. There was no way it could stay there between future snowstorms and threats of missteps. But for the present, it gave us a start.

The new solar panel resting on a corner of the deck

As my unplanned garden happily grew and I started harvesting lettuce, I had to admit Adam was right. For the first time as an adult, gardening was fun and easy. The four raised beds provided just enough space to grow a variety of plants from tomatoes to peppers, eggplants to asparagus. Even the rhubarb saved from an old farmhouse had a small spot. The size was manageable with few weeds. I took five minutes every weekend to tend it and kept a dream garden. I was charmed.

We'd been warned that insulated yurts were "flashy" as far as heating and cooling. The high tech insulation reflected heat in when the stove was going. If the heat source turned off, there was nothing to hold in the warmth. The summer quickly proved this was not an altogether worrisome thing. The dark sided yurt had full sun exposure. Despite the cream-colored top, temperatures would soar over 80 degrees even if outside it was only in the 70's. But as the sun fell to the ridge west of us, Maine's temperate climate took over. By early evening the yurt would cool off enough for a comfortable night's sleep. Mornings sometimes had a chill, although that faded as July progressed towards August.

The attributes of the insulation gave Adam an idea. He bought some extra insulation. Early one Thursday evening, he had me empty our icebox so he could line it with the thin sheets of insulation. I was for anything that kept the ice going a little bit longer and dropped the temperatures even a degree colder. I was adapting to the small size of the fridge, learning to buy little and use quickly. Besides that, our antique icebox worked surprisingly well. As long as we remembered to change the ice and empty the water.

Antique ice box with NASA designed insulation

However, neither of us were that fond of the solar shower. The small bag didn't hold that much water. If Adam wanted to shave, which he usually took care of in the shower, the water wasn't hot or plentiful enough. The second person often faced insufficient water, leaving the options of refilling with cold water or boiling water on the stove. When you are hot and tired after a long summer day, dealing with overuse of available shower water was a test of marriage vows. Not to mention that summer residents were migrating up the hill beyond the yurt. Suddenly showering in a bikini felt a little too exposing.

Our future goal was to buy a propane 'on demand' hot water heater. But first we needed to build a bathroom area in the yurt. Not to mention that the cost of even a small instant hot water heater was nearly $500. We both felt financially tapped out after how much the solar panel and batteries put on the credit card.

We needed a solution to at least gain some privacy. Looking over scrap lumber, I decided there was enough to build an outside shower stall. As I had with the outhouse, I spent hours pouring over elaborate designs for a changing area, interesting weaves of material to create screens, and different elevations in decking height so that the floor of the changing area wouldn't be flooded by the shower. It was quite a vision. It would also take weeks to build and required far more lumber than was available.

I pushed aside my daydreams and got practical. It just needed to work. With Adam's help, I pulled up a pallet that had come with the yurt parts and leveled it just below an exposed piece of granite bedrock twenty feet below the yurt. The spot was hidden from the road by trees and the slope of the hill. With only two long 2x4s and odds and ends of scrap lumber from other projects or from yurt packaging, I put together four corner posts connected by an overhead 'X.' To compensate for the shorter posts, I rested them on the rock ledge so they only needed to be four feet high. The back two posts I screwed into the pallet which I planked with scrap decking, leaving gaps for water drainage.

There was enough scrap lumber that I fashioned a seat in the shower and four corner selves big enough for soap, razors, and shampoo. I put a platform in the center of the 'X' to hang the solar shower on, though I could barely reach it. There was just enough extra lumber that I could connect the sides of the shower at the top and bottom on three sides. The screening to block chance views was going to have to be organic.

Adam caught me thinning a stand of spry saplings and screwing the stout limbs horizontally to the shower. He caught on quickly to my plan. Together we cut bracing and then wove leafy branches between the cross pieces. The shower took on a jungle appearance. Inside a quiet refuge of leaves above a moss covered stone above the wooden deck grew. The shower had turned out far better than I imagined.

For the open side, we ran an old shower curtain on a pole. It had to be weighted down so as not to flip open in a breeze. With the addition of a few convenient limbs to hang bathrobes and towels, the shower was ready for the solar water bag. Only that isn't what we used.

Adam had taken another run by the local green energy store. There amid the many on-demand hot water options lay one for outdoor use. It was less than $70. It needed water pressure going into it, but not much. And there were a variety of options to try to get it to work with low pressure. He bought it and brought it home while the shower was still being assembled.

A friend gave us a rain barrel. We'd hoped to use it to collect water off the yurt but the cost of the gutter system had derailed that idea. Now, Adam carted the rain barrel up the hill behind the yurt and shower and filled it with a hose from his parents' house. The outlet was located near the bottom of the barrel, so between the fifty gallons sitting above the spigot and the fall in height, the pressure was enough - just. It took some rereading of the instructions, turning of internal screws, and playing with max/min pressure versus temperature settings. All the adjustments were worth every frustrated second when we felt hot water pounding from the included shower head. It was nirvana.

I no longer had to shower the minute I arrived home. Now I could relax on the deck and wait until dusk. Cool breezes would sweep along my calves as I stood under water that felt limitless compared to the tiny solar shower. I could nudge the heat up or down. I could turn it off to shave my legs and be protected from wind and prying eyes. And best of all, I could shower naked.

The need for a changing room proved unnecessary. Adam or I would switch to a bathrobe and walk to the shower with a towel. The shower stall was big enough that I could stand to the side while the water warmed up. For Adam, who worked from home, the shower proved useful anytime of day. With the flick of a switch, he could turn off the propane. In our yurt life which did not include air conditioning, frequent dousings of cool water kept him going as summer progressed.

The outside shower with the instant hot water heater on the side – it doesn't look like much but it was heaven!

All the shower construction gave Adam one further idea. The solar panel placement on the deck was nearly perfect but for the railings. Musing about how to reduce the railing shadow, he realized he didn't need to get rid of the railing; he needed to move the solar panel to the sunny side. Adam took the last of the good lumber and made a support frame that the panel fit onto. Using hefty bolts rather than fragile screws and two heavy duty hinges, he attached the frame to the deck. The far edge was supported with one post. The slope of the ground was a good match to the post so that the frame could be lowered or raised with its one support to match the angle of the panel to the sun. For around $20 in hardware, Adam created a functional support frame for the solar panel.

Our very simple solar panel frame and support

We'd made it through our second month in the yurt. Improvements came quickly so that by the end we had not only solar power but an outdoor shower. Cooking was still akin to something we'd perform while camping, but with summer heat settling over Maine neither of us wanted to eat much anyway. The hottest month was ahead of us. And during it, we needed to start thinking of the looming winter.

— Autumn

> *"Damn perverted neighbors, we're gonna have to go all camo on them to hide our all natural shower!!"*
>
> - Adam: 20 July 2010

Finances were the number one reason we sold the house to follow this dream. The idea of actually going back into debt to pay for it was painful. The idea that we would pay it off easily is a nasty trap that would eventually keep us trapped. Unfortunately at the time we had priorities. The biggest of those was actually setting up the yurt to be independent and make it livable.

In selecting a location for the yurt we made a poor decision. We placed it at the edge of a field where it would be hit with sun from dawn until about 4:30pm during the summer. While the roof was white, the walls were dark green. The yurt baked in the sun. Given the option to do it again, we would have placed it squarely in the forest and protected from the sun. The location was set though, and we had to make it cool. A fan was necessary.

As we settled in, one big thing I did was upgrade the icebox fridge by adding reflect-ex insulation. This helped some, although thinking back there were other things that could have improved it more. Like just using a well insulated ice chest. A wooden antique box full of zink and who knows what will never equal modern materials.

My days were spent trying to figure out solutions to problems be it the water pressure for the shower or the electrical demands for the yurt. It seems there was no set method to really do anything and everyone had an idea on what was correct. While most solutions work, each option has its benefits and every problem is unique in its own way. Even once a problem was solved, I would continue thinking about ways to improve it. It was a constant and enjoyable challenge.

The solar battery bank and controller next to a window to help vent gasses

The shower was a unique problem. The yurt sat in an area where it afforded a nice view, but the drawback was that it was very visible, out in the sun, and with an old road passing within 50 feet, locals on ATVs and seasonal residents would drive by to gawk. Being a conservative town, we were "damn hippies" living in a "tent" and everyone had to swing by for a look. This parade made showering rather difficult so building a private bath was very important. Once it was completed we had what we needed, though the prospect of the coming winter worried me.

— Adam

STAR SHOWERS
AUGUST 2010

*"I've always wanted to see the Perseids. Somehow I
never have. By the time evening rolled around in early
August, I'd take my shower, think about sticking my head
outside the house, then go to bed. This year, it was different."*
- Autumn: 13 August 2010

A ugust dawned with sweltering heat. The hot air sat
stagnant over coastal Maine, barely dipping into the
seventies even at night. Even with the fan on full tilt, the
temperature in the yurt only felt comfortable after midnight. We
began to spend a lot of time outside in the shade.

A new weekend ritual began to form. After an early breakfast,
I'd make some extra coffee and boil eggs. The coffee went into a
jar next to the ice in the antique icebox. The eggs were shelled,
packed in a container, and dropped in our fridge as well. We would
get as much sorting done from our containers of bins in the shed
as we could before the afternoon temperatures became too much.
At that point, I'd make egg salad and turn the coffee into a non-ice

version of iced coffee. We'd pack up some magazines, put on swim suits, grab the two panting pups, and head to the lake for the afternoon, taking our picnic lunch along with us.

Down by the shore and in the shade, the temperature was often cool enough that swimming wasn't a necessity, just something to do. We'd swim off the dock while the dogs hunted frogs along the shore. Less work got done, but I couldn't have been happier. I've always loved water and grew up with a swimming pool in the side yard. I never thought we swam enough in Maine during the summer. Now every day involved water. Every hot night without an air conditioner was worth the discomfort just to spend hours floating during the day.

After dinner, which we'd begun to eat on the deck using a folding table and the two chairs we had in the yurt, we'd often head back to the shed. Adam's mother was planning on having a yard sale and invited us to join in. We had a 12-foot by 16-foot shed full of bins and furniture to sort through to get ready.

Even with only three months in the yurt and most belongings having been packed for six to eight months before that, our idea of what was essential had changed. Even books which I had once considered a large part of my life felt superfluous. Did I really need to hold onto a book I'd picked up for a dollar and hadn't really enjoyed reading? I was never going to have a library like one in an English manor house. Adam and I both felt ready to let things go. Which is good. Adam wanted to work on the motorcycle he bought in New Mexico in March in the shed this winter. It needed to be emptied within the next two months.

The first day of the yard sale was August 7th. We still weren't ready. Items like my old bed, extra dressers, and desks are easy. Adam and I hauled out the big things to his parents' driveway and onto tarps laid out around the shed. We put a small cluster of items we'd like to keep under a tarp. As people came to see what we had, we continued to haul out more bins, open them up, look through them, and usually transferred 99% of the contents over to a tarp to be sold. The agreement was that anything not sold by the end of August would be carted off to Goodwill. Nothing would be returned to storage.

There were clothes, second-hand scuba gear we'd never used, coats, tools, an old snowmobile, a boat with outboard engine, and furniture including my old art desk, chairs, and pieces of my childhood bedroom set. Every once in a while a moment of sentimentality washed over one of us. We'd sigh, maybe put something in the keep pile, but usually we'd cherish the memory, knowing it would last even if what had spawned it was gone. We no longer had the room for our lives to be about stuff.

As the stack of bins in the shed became less, we had more people start sticking their heads in to see what hadn't come out yet. The tarp over the furniture we were keeping would be lifted by the very bold even after we'd said nothing in that pile was for sale. A few people routinely came back and asked what else we had in the shed and if they could look through it to see if there was anything they wanted. The answer that we hadn't sorted through anything in the shed yet only seemed to increase their interest. With long days, warm temperatures, and lots of people looking over our belongings, annoyance set in. Adam or I would take a break, leaving the other solo to respond to questions with one word answers.

A small collection of the many things, including furniture, put out at the yard sale

We'd laugh later in the coolness of evening about the person who thought $5 was too much for a nearly new crockpot or the guy who walked around the back of the shed, through poison ivy, to see if we'd hidden anything good out of sight. Though I was happy to see our pile of belongings reduced to something manageable, I also saw the weekends of yard sales as a huge waste of time. It was summer in Maine. I'd sold the house to gain free time. I wanted to hike, camp, ride my motorcycle, pull out the kayaks. I consoled myself that those things would happen in time.

Obviously our old lives did not end with the sale of the house. We still had a lot of stuff to do to lighten the burden of once having owned a house and living via credit card and material goods. But every afternoon while I haggled over the $2 price tag of some former appliance, which would make me stand my ground just to be perverse, I'd think the day that we packed everything up and dropped it off at Goodwill couldn't come soon enough.

The best consolation for the long hot sale days was ice cream. With only primitive refrigeration, we had no way to keep something as fragile as ice cream around the yurt. I tended to buy blocks of ice, so even ice cubes were a rare commodity that was enjoyed while it was around. A bag of ice cubes enlivened a day with frosty drinks. Going out for ice cream was an event.

We would wrap up the sale a little early when people dropping by became scarce. In the bright late afternoon, we'd head out in the Jeep to one of the three local ice cream shacks. Summers in Maine are populated by seasonally open ice cream stands, the sort you have to drive or ride a bike to. Expensive compared to going to the store and buying a gallon of ice cream, they were an indulgence well worth while when the store was half an hour away and you had no way to store a gallon anyway.

Besides, the ice cream stand was only five minutes down the road and then we could swing by the lake to stick our feet in the cool water as we licked our dripping cones. Even the dogs got in on the deal with the puppy special sundays that came with sugar free vanilla and a dog bone on top. Sitting side-by-side on the dock with bare legs swirling in water while licking massive cones, with two dogs rapidly licking a to-go cup of ice cream on the shore, we could have been two kids on a summer childhood romance instead of two thirty-somethings downsizing our lives to fit into 500 square feet.

Despite the heat and its spawned crankiness or moments of idleness, it was time to think towards winter beyond more than emptying the shed. During June when Adam was away, we'd had a few days so cool and damp that a friend had lent me a small propane heater. I'd accepted it with a laugh.

Keeping cool with the pup

"Now that you loaned it to me, it won't get cold again until fall."

The statement had proven prophetic and I'd never so much as found a propane tank to hook it to. Although the early August nights were hot, we knew we were mere weeks from having temperatures dip into the fifties at night. Fall came quickly this far north. We had to start thinking about how we'd heat our little round abode.

Adam researched wood stoves. We'd owned a variety by this point in our home heating days: Vermont Castings, a Jotul insert, and no-name brands as well. We'd both grown up with steel stoves rather than cast iron. Out of all the brands, we kept coming back to Morso. One of the oldest stove makers in business, this Denmark brand was energy efficient in ways I'd never considered in a wood stove before. The downside was the cost, over twice a comparable

Jotul and three times what a no name model would be. We weren't really sold on any one model or brand. We agreed that we just needed to find one that would work.

We had the conundrum of needing a stove with a small woodbox so that we didn't heat ourselves out of the 500-square-foot yurt, but one that had a long enough burn time we wouldn't be up every four hours adding wood to keep the coals going. A flat top that made cooking on the stove an option was a huge plus.

We kept an eye out for used stoves in the local "For Sale" publications and called a few with potential Jotuls and Morsos. Nothing panned out: fire boxes were cracked, stoves were rusted, or the seals were gone. Then Adam stumbled upon an out of the way stove shop having a summer sale during the heat of August. He came home to tell me he'd put money down on a Morso that was 50% off.

The size was perfect. It could take 18-inch logs, which was the average size to buy locally. With a large glass front and ornamental knotwork on the sides, it was attractive. It had an ash pan to make cleanout easy, a flat top to make cooking possible, fire bricks to retain heat, and even extra cadmium in the iron to help it hold heat longer. The burn time was listed at eight hours. And with the sale, it was ours for $900, which was the same amount as the Jotul we'd all but decided to purchase.

Adam brought home the wood stove on a hot August day. He settled it into its spot between the table and the futon where it looked out of place in the bright sunshine flowing through the top dome and open windows. There was still plenty of work to do to install the stove. We needed to put in a chimney support, buy the chimney pieces, and cut a hole through the yurt wall - both the fabric and lattice. But considering it was August and over 80 degrees, just having the wood stove seemed enough. It was also a good reminder we needed to order wood.

As the evening of August 12th rolled around, staying out on the deck and drinking a hard apple cider just seemed part of the normal flow of our lives. It had been a hot day. When I came home from work, the yurt was baking inside. Normal routine was to change the ice blocks and empty the water to the icebox. We drank iced tea in the shade of the back corner of the deck where we could admire the healthy plants in our little garden.

The new wood stove – purchased, but not needed, in August!

Dinner, besides being made towards dusk, was prepared on the grill as much as possible. Simple meals involving lettuce from the garden or grilled shrimp along with camp style fresh bread made with garden herbs was getting us through the hot days. Our current propane grill had a one-burner stovetop. Although I'd feel badly heating up a huge grill to cook shrimp, I loved the outdoor stove option.

From news reports, I knew that night was the height of the Perseids meteor shower. Adam and I dawdled on the deck, backs to the railing and watched the night sky. I'd always wanted to watch a meteor shower.

At the old house, we'd often slept in the sunporch. I'd try to wake up after midnight, fumble for my glasses, and look for shooting stars through the skylights. I never saw anything. A few times I'd even walked outside but there had been no comfortable place to sit and the surrounding forest blocked a wide view of the sky.

Without even putting in an effort, the night flowed into the perfect opportunity to watch the Perseids unfold. Adam saw the first faint trace across the heavens. Then I finally saw my first Perseid shooting star zip a white line against the black night. We watched for nearly an hour, talking softly and exclaiming over the brightest or longest meteors.

As we were thinking of calling it a night, one large streak arced above us. Just as it began to fade, the meteor exploded in a ball of light and hurtled brilliantly onward. It took a few more seconds for the second stage shooting star to fade. After that we were hooked into watching another fifteen minutes. There wasn't anything close to the dazzling display we'd just seen and eventually we both decided it was time for bed. I still had to go to the office in the morning. But we both kept an eye to the night sky as we brushed our teeth and took the dogs out one last time.

Afternoon swims and the Perseids made the long weekend days spent hosting a yard sale survivable. The weather was warm enough that riding a motorcycle in full gear didn't sound like too much fun. Camping would have been a nice getaway, but we were still unpacking boxes and locating all of our gear. I settled down and admitted we needed to finish sorting our belongings. Otherwise we'd likely leave them in storage for eternity. Reaching the back of the shed became a goal.

During the heat, we found our first real problem with the antique icebox. I was generally disappointed that ice would last a maximum of two days and that was being generous. The second day the melted block barely kept anything cold. On the hot days, I was changing the ice daily. But it was tolerable. I could buy blocks of ice cheap and we toyed with the idea of using the freezer from the old house which was currently kept in Adam's parents' garage.

But one morning I noticed that no water was in the drip tray. The floor was a bit damp so I mopped it up and figured I'd misaligned the tray with the outlet so melted water had hit the floor. No big deal, so I went to work. Adam emailed later to say the floor next to the fridge was soaked. There was still no water in the drip tray. He couldn't figure out what was going wrong and so put down towels. We tackled the issue together when I got home.

The first thing we did was empty out everything in the fridge. As we lifted the zinc platform out of the ice compartment, we realized what was wrong: slime mold. The temperature was warm enough that along with the wet and potential organic nutrients, a slime mold had grown across the bottom of the ice compartment. As more ice had melted onto it, it had flowed down the drainage hole and plugged it.

"They never mentioned that problem in the history books."

We both laughed. I cleaned out the mold and sprayed down the fridge with a cleaner containing bleach. Adam found a wire to flush out the drainage hole and within half an hour we were putting the fridge back together. Having to worry about slime mold was annoying, especially because it didn't smell. In a traditional fridge a pervasive smell warned when something had gone bad. Here there was only a minimal amount of water in the drip tray and some dampness on the floor to alert of a problem.

I tried to make cleaning the fridge a weekly habit, but there were times that the mold and I were not in sync. It would get ahead of me and block the drain, usually to be discovered by Adam during the day. We bought blue ice blocks that we could keep in the old freezer and wouldn't have the melt issue, but real ice worked the best. I froze water in tupperware containers, but there was condensation no matter what we used. I started looking forward to fall and cooler temperatures for a whole new reason: inhibiting slime mold growth.

Another new phenomenon were afternoon thunderstorms. We'd dealt with rain in the yurt before, having the top cover baptized while it was installed. The sound of rain on the yurt roof was a cross between a tin roof and a tent. The polyvinyl and insulation plus the polycarbonate dome transmitted the sound of a gentle sprinkle. We'd walked outside wearing raincoats due to the pounding raindrops only to find that it was barely drizzling and you could walk between rain drops.

Nothing quite prepared us for the sound of an afternoon deluge. It sounded like we'd parked the yurt under Niagara Falls. The torrent was so loud that if we were watching a movie we'd have to turn it off. The volume didn't go high enough to override the cascading rain. We'd just give up and watch the wild weather until the storm passed. We had to shout to hear each other even from a few feet apart, so we usually didn't talk beyond, "Want some tea?" Eventually that just turned into me lifting the kettle and looking at Adam, he'd nod and give me a thumb's up. I'd double check the desired beverage by holding up a coffee bag or a tea tin far enough apart to discern which he pointed at. We'd merrily sip our drinks while the sky opened up and cooled the earth.

Toward the end of the month searching the for sale ads on-line, Adam emailed me at work to say he'd found something on my wish list. The outhouse was working fine, but my heart was set on a

Sun Mar composting toilet. It would be something we could keep in the yurt once I'd built an inside bathroom. But like the solar powered fridge I liked, the price was high. At over $1400 for a new model and with the solar panel, batteries, wire, the ceiling fan and now a wood stove on the credit card, I contented myself with the outhouse. It was functional and had been spiffed up with an oak toilet seat and a fairly high tech ventilation shaft designed by Adam. Then Adam let me know he'd found a Sun Mar for $600 that was slightly used from a camp up north.

I gave the owner a call and found out the specifics. The wife had wanted a real septic system in the camp they'd purchased, but the previous owner had used the Sun Mar and it had worked great. They'd used it while the septic was being installed without a problem. It had been cleaned up, looked great, and could be mine for $600. We hit up an ATM and headed north in the Jeep.

The seller looked a little surprised that we wanted to haul the thing home in a Jeep Wrangler. But after folding and tumbling the rear seat, the composting toilet fit in perfectly. It just meant the two Cairn terriers had lost their seat and my lap had to suffice for the ride home. The Sun Mar was in great shape, came with instructions from someone who'd used it successfully, and was fiberglass instead of plastic like modern versions. I was thrilled with the find. We'd saved over $800. Adam still thought the outhouse was sufficient. I shrugged it off but reading through the instructions I did pause.

There were two things liable to cause a problem. The first was the version we'd purchased had an AC fan in the vent pipe instead of being the electric free model. We'd have to do some figuring and jury rigging to find a way to make it work for us. And the last note that made me bite my lip was the recommendation that the toilet needed to stay above 70 degrees. That was warm. Awfully warm when we hadn't even spent a winter in our yurt yet.

Adam and I pushed aside the worry for the moment. Though the specter of having a smelly toilet in our small living space lingered in my mind, that possibility was a ways off. It was only mid-August, we had no place to even install the toilet at the moment, we'd figure out the venting, plumbing, and heating when the time came to that. For now, we just needed to get our new discovery home and take the dogs swimming. The next day, we were going to finally hit the back of the shed and open the last of the bins from the old house. One more weekend of trying to sell our belongings and then we'd start packing everything remaining to take to Goodwill on the last weekend of August. Then we'd have to start getting serious about fall.

— Autumn

"Damn I wish we had placed this more in the shade, biggest mistake ever."

- Adam: 17 August 2010

Y ard sales are something I truly dislike. Some of my earliest memories were trips to Maine in a Jeep Cherokee. With each yard sale stop, my seating space shrank until I was wedged between bureaus or under a mattress. Then the trip was cut short due to money or room.

I was the son of a long line of antique dealers. Saturdays growing up were spent at yard sales, but I was tasked to sneak into the sheds or garages to rummage. Then every Sunday all summer was spent at flea markets selling to the collecting masses. Unlike many my age who grew relationships and gained experience at summer camp, Boy Scouts, or participated in sports, I sold antiques.

The benefit of cleaning out the storage shed was that I could create work space to restore the R80 G/S – it was small but it worked!

My childhood experiences made having a yard sale of my own and dealing with those career yard salers a very maddening experience. Not quite as bad as Stewart the rat, but still quite unpleasant. Like Autumn, I was happy to simply drop off my valuables to Goodwill for free rather than submit to some dealer to accept a third of what they would make the following day. August was a slow month and not just for the weekend reminders of my strange childhood.

The yurt was hot! Not the sort of warmth you can endure, but the sort of heat that makes pavement melt, brains boil, and elicits news reports of dogs suffering in cars sort of hot. It was terrible. One day sitting in the center of the yurt in a wet bathing suit, damp not from swimming but sweating, with the fan running full tilt and the dome open, I wondered how we'd survive. When night came, the biomass of furniture and floor insulation retained the heat well into the evening, keeping the yurt unpleasantly warm. These are things yurt manufacturers do not tell you. And why, if we were to do it again, we would place the yurt in a shaded hardwood grove so that it was sunny in the winter but shaded in the summer.

Autumn and the dogs keeping cool in the shade of the yurt

Rain though was a wonderful experience. The yurt was basically a big drum. Every external sound became amplified which in the case of rain was a magical thing to enjoy. The amplification came at a price though, being close to a road, all the road traffic could be clearly heard as if the traffic buzzed by on the other side of the fabric wall. From the softest loon cry on the lake to semi-trucks' blasting air brakes, we heard it all and had to live with the noise as well as enjoy the beauty.

— Adam

LOOKING TOWARD FALL
SEPTEMBER & OCTOBER 2010

"Truly hot weather is brief in Maine. Every blistering day, we'd tell ourselves in a mere handful of weeks we'd miss the warmth. Already the nights are cool enough for another blanket and the leaves are starting to change. The plants in the garden are just reaching peak production while the season is nearly over."

- Autumn: 6 September 2010

The hot weather cast a lethargy over Adam and me. Even though we'd managed to sort through all of our possessions in the storage shed and whittle our belongings down to 20 bins from the 90 we'd packed, we hadn't done any work on the yurt. We had a composting toilet with no place to put it, an outdoor shower that we could only use another month, and we'd never fully finished installing everything in the yurt kit back in June. It was time to get back to work.

The first unfinished chore was installing the perimeter blocking around the inside of the yurt. The yurt kit had come with two pallets of red pine to be cut to fit between each of the rafter support posts. The instructions from Pacific Yurts said to install them just below the rafters vertically. I'd seen posts from other yurt owners installing them horizontally to make four-inch shelves around the perimeter of the yurt. With only 500 square feet of space, any extra storage is a great option.

Being a circle, cutting the perimeter blocks to fit was not a simple matter of measuring the distance between rafters. For a good fit, each edge had to have an angled cut so that the straight board would fit in its piece of the round whole. The instructions recommended a 4% angle. I gave it a try and found that while it wasn't perfect, it was better than 5% or 3%.

On the weekend of September 4th, I got serious about finishing the blocking. Leaves on stressed trees had been changing since mid-August despite the heat. Now with temperatures hovering in the high seventies and the nighttime temperatures down to the fifties, it was beginning to feel like fall. We didn't want to store the two pallets of blocking under the yurt all winter. Besides, the blocking helped disperse the snow load, which would soon be a needed function.

I started slow, measuring between two rafters, making the cut, and then installing the block before going on to the next two rafters. By the time I'd finished five of the blocks, I started measuring the next three sections. Before I was halfway through, I wrote down the measurements to the rest of the rafters and went outside to spend quality time with the miter saw. I dropped off the correct block to its section as I went so as not to get confused. It almost worked.

When I came in and started installing in mass, I realized my mistake. Every fraction of an inch that the cut was off added up as the blocks were screwed into place. Since the rafters rested on a steel cable, they could slide to a new position even through the rafter supports were screwed to the floor and the lattice work. Across a few rafters, this sliding wasn't an issue as the gaps would be corrected when I measured the next section. Around half a yurt, I began to have problems.

There wasn't anything that couldn't be overcome. I had to switch blocks around. There were a few extra red pine boards that had come with the yurt, but not many. I never did resort to cutting a new piece of perimeter blocking, but my ability to use the power drill just enough to put two pieces of wood together without pulling them perfectly flush became very good. I made a mental note that the next time I worked on something circular not to take any big short cuts. Circles are fluid and need lots of attention.

The blocking was done in a day and before I'd even put the saws and power drill away, Adam was claiming half of them for his personal use. He found the odds and ends he used to keep on his dresser and began spreading them across his newly claimed territory. The field guides came out of storage and fit perfectly on the small shelves. Amused, I spread out some of the kitchen spices and butter dish to new homes up near the rafters. We were starting to make our tent a bit more of a home.

The horizontal shelves of the perimeter blocking already utilized!

With the renewed construction to encourage him, Adam decided to install the chimney support. The direction from Pacific Yurts suggested installing the chimney between two supports but the location of the deck versus the chimney made this difficult. In the end he purchased a 16-foot four by six-inch beam and had it delivered.

Adam cut a hole in the decking between two main deck supports and dug a deep hole underneath. After drilling holes through the four by six-inch beam and through the deck supports, he bolted the chimney support in place and then encased the base in concrete. It wasn't the recommended installation, but our chimney support was solid. The monolith support was ready early in the week of September 6th.

While I went to work that week, he continued with assembling the chimney pieces and tackling the part we were both nervous about: cutting a hole into the sidewall of our new yurt. Adam measured where the stove pipe needed to come out, following the recommendations of which pieces of lattice it should go through due to structure of the lattice wall, as well as distance from the rafter supports. He removed the 'X' of lattice and then faced making the cut through the sidewall and insulation.

The hole for the chimney through wall connection

The circle to be removed was to be two inches bigger than the six-inch stovepipe. It turned out that a dinner plate fit the diameter perfectly. Adam traced a circle off a plate and then cut it out with an xacto knife and a pair of scissors. After that, it was a matter of assembling the pieces of chimney and stove pipe, adding flashing, attaching everything to the stove, and sealing the outside so that water couldn't drip in and cause a problem.

Every day I came home a bit more was done. Finally on Friday the 10th, I got a picture emailed to me of a cheery little fire in the wood stove. He'd finished the installation and lit our first fire to test everything was sealed properly. The little Morso stove drafted beautifully and was pretty to watch. Only time would tell if the glass would be easy to keep clean and how much heat it would put off. For now in early September, fires would be sporadic affairs allowed to smolder down to ash.

First frost can come as early as mid-September in Maine. It was a nice year, cool but not quite cold. Nights were crisp and the wind kicked up. We grew used to the whispering scratch of falling leaves drifting across the yurt roof or the sharp tap of an acorn hitting the deck. Mornings were misty and gray. The honk of unseen geese filled the air as they left the lake at dawn to head south. The prehistoric sound of loons that had filled the nights all summer became less frequent, but would still cut through the dark as they echoed across the water and surrounding hills.

The temperature became cool enough that the warmer weather plants grew ragged. The eggplants stopped producing but the remaining fruit kept growing in the sun. Even the tomatoes didn't look quite ready to call it quits. My reluctant garden had become a small point of pride. I'd never managed green peppers much less eggplants at the old house. Now I had both as well as tomatoes and chard, herbs and zucchini.

It was fall but I wasn't ready to let the garden go. I started looking around for wood scrap to build a frame for plastic to keep off the first frost. I hobbled together a ramshackle frame that fell from the deck to the ground. Milky plastic could be thrown over it to protect the plants from cold and left on to help warm the plants in the morning.

The yurt in the fall with gardens covered

I now found myself showering in the dark when using the outdoor shower. Adam rigged a magnetic tap light to hang from a washer on the crossed overhead beams. He also took the extra plastic I used for the garden plants and encased the shower to cut down on the once refreshing breezes that had taken a nippier edge. To help hide the strange outdoor arrangement, he used some guille cloth accented with real branches to conceal our shower. The tap light didn't give away the latest cation, but the steam emitted from the hot water lofting into the cool air was a pretty good indicator that something was going on back there.

The plastic wrap topped with guille cloth bought us a few more months of showering, we figured. The walk back to the yurt could be cool, but it was less than 100 feet. While the water was on, the shower was heaven and the occasional breeze just accented the warmth more. Even the nights when the fall rains set in were not that bad. It never seemed to be raining too hard to make walking outside in a robe to take a shower an issue. It wasn't like we needed a raincoat and probably would have just run out naked if it'd come to that.

The rain did point out one of the first flaws with our new yurt. We'd placed the door for a good view of the lake far below us on our hill. It also placed the door directly in the path of the heaviest of storms. As torrential winds hammered into the door, water seeped underneath. It wasn't a lot of water, but did require a towel. We tried weather-stripping, but it didn't stick well to the oiled wood of the door. For the time being we shrugged. A towel worked. Fall storms wouldn't last long and snow would be a lot less messy.

I'd spent time over the summer months designing the "snubbed nose wedge" that would house the indoor shower and the composting toilet. It would look like a piece of pie with the tip cut off, taking a slice out of our home's roundness. I wasn't one to build walls in our tiny home without using every possible inch for storage. Instead of usual lumber walls comprised of 2x4s, I planned to use 2x12s and make built-in shelves out of every nook and cranny. One outside wall would host kitchen "cabinets" and my counter, the short front would be for the flat screen TV and a media center, while the far side with the door to the bathroom would be a library. Up above would be extra storage.

That was the gist of the idea. I played around with configurations, potential closets, and how to incorporate a pocket door. We measured the shower stall we were thinking of buying only to find out the walls to the corner stall we liked wouldn't fit under the ceiling height necessitated by the yurt walls. Ideas to solve this issue were tossed out and discarded. I couldn't figure an easy way to accommodate the hardware for a pocket door and still have enough headroom so Adam wouldn't clock his forehead every time he walked in or out.

It was frustrating, especially considering Adam became more against the idea of building something that would break up the perfect circle of the yurt. I finally decided to keep it simple and build to the height I needed without a pocket door. I ignored Adam's desire to not have any interior walls, but did agree to make the future bathroom as small as possible - no closets or extra space inside the wedge. It would all be functional and minimal. We'd have to make our own walls to the shower and just buy the corner tub to the shower stall. It would save money and to save even more I ordered 2x4's with just 2x12 beams for the floor and lintels of the three walls. The wood came on September 24th.

It was a sunny Saturday on the 10th of October as I pulled out all the saws and put the lumber on the deck. I rearranged the yurt to give me working space, moving the table out of the way, while Adam visited his parents. He came back, took a look around and left again. I was on my own with a handful of designs drawn into my journal and a lot of lumber.

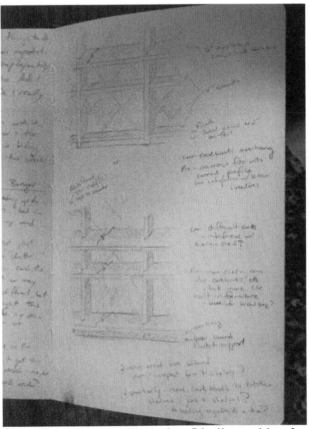

I'd draw designs with notes before I built anything for the yurt

Adam's adamant dislike for the project gave me pause. Was it really worth this much friction to build the wedge? I thought about our options. He'd suggested we shower over at his parents' house for the winter. The kitchen set-up of the old workbench worked somewhat. What finally made up my mind was my strong independent streak. We had owned two houses and I disliked depending on someone else for basic living necessities. But it was a test of my abilities. I'd designed this wedge with built-in bookcase walls. I'd drawn lines on the floor for the last month measuring out where the shower would fit, where we'd need walls, and how small the space could be.I've always liked the idea of working in wood. Ever since college when I'd worked in a theater department to build sets to gain certification in both wood and machine shop, I had wanted to build things. With the houses we'd owned, I had fixed things. I had installed doors, tile, and built a wine and spice rack. But I'd never really built a house until the yurt and I hadn't designed it. I hadn't built walls until I put together the storage shed under the yurt and then the outhouse. This inside room was the next step. It was a piece of furniture that served as a room divider. It was also going to be assembled with screws and could come apart, in case we moved or in case we hated it. I had the wood. I really wanted to see if I was capable of this. I got to work.

By the time Adam wandered back, I had one wall on the floor ready to be lifted into place. The angled piece would be structurally strong, once I actually got it upright. But the heavy 2x12 top piece with only 2x4s and screws between it and the base was proving too flimsy to move upright. I was starting to think I'd failed before I even got started.

Despite his opposition, Adam's problem solving nature took hold. He took an uncut 2x4 and put it under the whole airy wall. Together we lifted the first wall into place, using the extra 2x4 as support. He still frowned but he helped lift the other two walls into place as I quickly finished their assembly, having cut the wood to length that morning.

We stood back and viewed the assembled wedge. It was nearly eight feet along the two sides and the flat front was four feet. Built almost perfectly to the design in my journal, I was at least happy to see I could build something. It was intrusive into the yurt, but not horribly. Neither of us could quite decide what we thought of it. But it was also late afternoon, the yurt was a mess and the day had been both physically and mentally trying. I scraped together a surface to cook on as we decided to call it a day.

The wedge taking shape

It took a while to get motivated Sunday morning. The open frame of the bathroom wedge and the disorder it made in the location of furniture in our 480-square-foot yurt was impossible to ignore. We started the process of rearranging. The kitchen table, once located where the new kitchen would be was moved to where the futon had been located. The futon was swung directly across from the flat front of the wedge, which would one day house our flat screen TV. However, where the futon was now located was where the current kitchen resided. So the kitchen needed to be disassembled.

Adam pointed out that if I had some extra wood, the legs to the workbench I'd been using as a kitchen cook surface could be narrowed. With some adjustment, we pulled the metal legs together and managed to raise the height a few inches. With some short 2x4s as cross braces, I used a leftover 2x12 and a 2x4 to create a narrow custom counter top to run along the exterior of the new wedge.

When I finally had money to buy more lumber, I would build the shelves and bookcases between the supports of the wedge, making my kitchen much more functional. But for now, the long counter top with space for the two-burner Coleman camp stove we'd upgraded to and space for food prep felt familiar.

With the yurt rearranged we sat down and took in the change. We'd had some debate on where to put things in our suddenly rearranged living space, and a few words on if certain items were even necessary. But looking now at the walls I'd built and the beginnings of a true kitchen area, we both were surprised to realize we liked it. The yurt was no longer something that had come out of a kit and assembled to instructions. We'd taken a leap and begun to change it into our vision of a yurt. It was beginning to feel like home.

— Autumn

> *"My dog is blind, it's important to have a round house,*
> *both internal and external so that he can find his way out ...*
> *AND in."*
>
> - Adam: 4 October 2010

One of the reasons I wanted the yurt was because of the illusion of mobility, as well as the roundness. I embraced my circular home. Tibetan color scarves were placed at each cardinal point. The door was south, the fire north, the bed west for end of day, and the kitchen east for new beginnings.

Imagine my dismay when Autumn wished to put a big wooden ark in the middle of my sanctuary. The installation was the beginning of the end. I was not interested in assisting with this destruction of my dream. Even if it was unfortunately necessary to live there. We couldn't shower outside all winter.

Outside showers in the fall were an interesting affair. From a physics standpoint, hot water freezes sooner than cold. We showered in the evening and one of my concerns of was that the water would freeze within the manifold of our water heater as it was already freezing in the hose. Every night involved draining the heater and hoping there was no water remaining. The wedge which would contain the shower was needed sooner than later. But how would we keep the water going all winter? Right now the water for the shower was stored outside. There were a lot of problems to solve.

Fire was a personal necessity for us. One of the best parts of living in Maine is the normality of wood fires. Naturally, we did not hesitate to have a wood stove in the yurt. Many manufacturers place the stove in the center with the chimney going through the roof near the center dome. I do not like this option for a variety of reasons so we settled for a wall vent. Cutting a hole in the side of the house, through the lattice and polyvinyl, was not taken lightly and was rather unnerving. I had a template, but unlike with wood it's hard to board a fabric wall up if I made a mistake. So I measured ten times and cut once ... very slowly.

Mounting the chimney proved a challenge. Not only did it have to extend above the highest point of the yurt within ten feet to meet code, I had to lift it up and lock it into place against a flexible 4x6 with a rickety ladder. I managed the feat with a strong dose of fear, one of them lingered.

The installed chimney

Hot embers and plastic do not mix. I worried sparks coming out of the chimney would land on the roof, resulting in an ongoing problem of holes. Given this fear I made a point to keep the chimney clean with the ability to sweep it from the bottom. The idea of snow on the roof to create another layer of protection made me look forward to winter.

— Adam

A FLURRY OF CONSTRUCTION
NOVEMBER & DECEMBER 2010

*"I look around the small space we have. It is too
cluttered with stuff and we still have possessions in bins. My
family keeps asking me what I want for Christmas. For a
long time I couldn't think of anything to tell them, then I
realized there was one thing I really wanted."*

- Autumn: 10 November 2010

Т he last time we showered outside was on November 1st. It
was cold. Frost had killed off the garden. The trees were
bare. The damp walk between the shower and warm yurt
was chilling. But it was the last outside shower. As Adam put it, we
could say we showered outside in Maine in November. At least it
hadn't snowed.

Despite finishing the frame to the wedge on October 10th, we
didn't buy the shower tub and wall paneling for a week. We wanted
to put off the expense as long as possible, but the rate at which our
nightly outside showers became cold made it apparent that we
couldn't delay completing the inside shower for long.

Finally, as keeping the gardens covered in their fragile shell of plastic became a full-time affair even though the tomatoes and eggplants finally succumbed to the cold nights, Adam began the inside shower installation. The tub was installed and a hole drilled for the drain. We plumbed the outlet to go into a gravel seep for gray water. To solve the problem of supplying enough water to meet the needs of a shower during the winter, a 16-gallon cistern was installed in the 12-inch kitchen walls. It was a perfect fit between the supports.

We added an inline pump to boost pressure since we wouldn't have a 50-gallon container of water with gravity pressure as an added boost inside the yurt. That had to be wired as well. With the drilling, plumbing, and wiring everything wasn't in place until the end of October. Just to be his stubborn self, Adam didn't take down the instant hot water heater from the outdoor shower and install it until November 2nd. The garden had frozen and died before the inside shower was operational.

After the first inside shower, which seemed far too easy to simply undress and walk into a small room and flip a switch, I couldn't complain. The hot water without bone chilling breezes was lovely. The pressure was better than either house we'd once owned, not to mention the houses we'd grown up in. The shower was not pretty. It didn't look finished being just a 39" by 39" corner tub, two walls of plastic board, a wooden shelf above the board on one wall, and a not so perfectly strung shower curtain. All the plumping was exposed and the on/off switch was a toggle located just outside the shower curtain on the wall. But the shower worked quite well.

With the shower finished and location determined, I brought up the composting toilet. It fit well in its planned space. But we hit a problem. We'd wanted one window in the bathroom, but we'd also wanted the bathroom to remain as small as possible. I'd built the kitchen wall with enough room that the shower would fit against it without covering a window, which also kept all the running water in the same space if I ever wanted to install a faucet that ran off the instant hot water heater.

Looking through the wedge "door" to the inside shower

The location of the shower against the yurt wall meant the opposite wall of the bathroom wedge was just beyond a window. To install the composting toilet's vent pipe we couldn't go through the yurt side with a 90-degree angle like we'd hoped. We would have to go through the roof.

Neither of us liked the idea of putting a hole in our new roof. We researched the method and how to seal around the hole, but we were both nervous about it. The yurt roof moved with big gusts. How would the potential friction and sliding work against a fixed pipe? How could it not leak? Plus the vent pipe for the electric model came out the back and was only a two-inch pipe. For the non-electric vent, the pipe was supposed to come out the top and be four inches. Adam found instructions on how to drill a hole for a new vent pipe and bought the parts. But we put them on top of the toilet and stopped. Worry nagged us. There was too much jury rigging going on and it was making the process very complicated.

As the nights and days became colder, we kept the fire going full-time. The yurt easily stayed a toasty 70 degrees-plus during the day, hotter if the sun was out to help warm things up. We often had to dampen the stove completely. At night with the stove dampened, inside temperatures could drop to the low 60s. There were still coals in the morning, but the yurt would be chilly until the fire warmed things up. It suggested to me that in the dead of winter, we'd need to do more than dampen the fire and throw some blankets on the bed. One of us would have to throw a log or two in overnight.

The dogs LOVED the wood stove

It was the nighttime temperatures that were the final straw for the composting toilet. Our instructions said to keep the toilet above 70 degrees. Between the low nighttime temperatures in the yurt and a vent pipe that was the wrong type that would have to go through the roof, I caved in. Adam was already fine with the idea of just using the outhouse. I finally admitted that the idea of the composting toilet was not working. I agreed to the outhouse for the winter. The composting toilet went under the yurt for storage until we decided if the outhouse would work permanently. The decision to keep the composting toilet would be made in the spring.

With the holidays approaching, family started asking us what we wanted for Christmas. We were both stumped. We still had a few bins in the shed, which Adam wanted out so that we could store the bikes and he could begin to restore the R80. As we sealed bins that were safe to freeze with duct tape to keep out mice and moved them to a safe storage spot beneath the yurt for the winter, I pondered the question: What did I want for the holidays?

I ran through ideas of coats, skis, hiking, and motorcycle gear without coming up with anything that seemed worth the problem of storage. I needed to finish sorting through what I had packed away, and didn't have a place to unpack anyway. How could I ask for more? Which is when I finally realized there was one thing I wanted above all others.

Ever since finishing the wedge, I'd started drawing layouts for shelves. I'd measured depths and arrangements. I knew exactly how many feet of what length board I needed. It was a couple hundred dollars. I wanted the project done, but I was loathe to go further in debt to do it. I had known that this first year was going to be expensive. We had to buy the yurt and set up a complete household. But I hated seeing the credit card bill. We seemed to need things and purchase them far faster than we were making payments. Buying wood had become a wish list item. And that was exactly what my family was asking me to give them. So I finally told everyone what I wanted for Christmas: lumber.

Family came through like a charm. I had the money to go pick up the length and widths I needed the weekend before Thanksgiving. As other folks were preparing turkey and stuffing, I was pulling out the miter saw.

The days were still bright and although I needed to wear an old coat to cut wood on deck, there was no snow as I began work on November 25th. I picked up where I left off and that was framing in the top loft area of the shower wedge. Up until now the overhead view when taking a shower had been the rising yurt rafters. Now I placed carefully measured 2x4s on end to make a ceiling with a six-inch overhang on the three sides.

Building the frame of the wedge had given me confidence. This time I carefully measured lengths to get the most out of a board and also buy the cheapest lengths available. Twelve-foot 2x4s tapered to eight-footers in the front. I worked out a way to cut two 4x8 sheets of plywood to work as the loft floor. Adam finally got to see my careful measuring and cutting that had gained me the extra wood to panel the outhouse out of the wood he'd ordered for the storage area under the yurt. For the final piece of the loft, I cut trim boards to cover the 2x4 rafter ends. The wedge was beginning to take on a finished look.

The loft was an immediate hit with Adam. If there were any lingering doubt over the construction of the wedge in our circular home, it was gone the minute he climbed the stepladder and perched himself in the new loft. It was his nest and he wasn't going to give it up. I was nervous about my airy wedge, but seeing it hold Adam's weight made me feel better. The shelves set between the rafter supports would only provide more stability. It was time to get them done as well.

I built the media center for the short front of the wedge first. Above it and facing the shower, I made a medicine style cabinet that would be for storage in the bathroom. Before the weekend had ended, I'd built the first two kitchen shelves as well. Both ran full length from floor support to ceiling and so were fairly easy to build. The worst part was taking apart the kitchen counter to install them. The part that I'd thought would be hard, making an 'X' in one to serve as a wine rack, ended up being the fastest and easiest part of the project. I offered to make custom wine racks for everyone once I realized how simple the cut was to make in each half of the board. When they slid together, were inserted to their space, and spread into the 'X' of the rack, I was simply tickled. It was one of the best Christmas presents I'd ever received.

By the end of Sunday night as I put away tools and swept up sawdust, the front of the wedge was covered in wainscot paneling and the flat screen TV was hung in its place above. The media center housed the DVD player, my old stereo, and shelves of DVDs. The medicine cabinet was filled with creams and aspirin, toothpaste and Q-tips. As I made dinner, Adam climbed into the loft and peered down at me cooking below him.

The wedge with the front paneled and kitchen shelves including the wine rack – note the "in wall" 16 gallon cistern behind the propane tank

"Smells good."

"So much for using the loft for storage." Adam stuck his tongue out at me.

I was just happy that the food was out of reach, at least for the moment. Otherwise he was most likely going to stay up there. I kept use of the two kitchen shelves to a minimum, knowing I'd be disrupting things again to finish the shelves. But I did unpack my small hoard of wine. Twelve full size bottles and the four narrow speciality wines and cordials fit into my tiny 'X.' I was dancing around the yurt despite feeling sore from the days of cutting wood on the deck and drilling together boards. Monday at the office sounded a bit like a nice break.

I didn't get back to building the remainder of the shelves for a couple of weeks. With holiday shopping and poor weather moving in, finding time to construct was scarce. Adam did insulate two of the windows with the kits we'd purchased from Pacific Yurts. Made out of the same insulation material with a cream inner cover as the yurt walls, the window kits clipped into the window harness and then zipped into place by closing the flap on the cloth windows. We gained heat but lost light.

The type of insulation that was used in the yurt got Adam thinking. Initially, worried about cold winter months ahead, much less the ones we were experiencing, he wanted to order more window kits. But days are already short in Maine during December. Sealing off more light even for warmth didn't feel like a healthy idea. We'd actually taken down the two window awnings not only to protect them but because they blocked the pale winter light. Instead of sealing off more windows with kits, Adam gathered up all the large bubble wrap he could find. He taped the sheets of wrap together and put these over the three remaining windows. The result blocked visibility but not light. It wasn't the fanciest solution, but it worked.

All the taping inspired one more insulation idea for Adam. We'd been staring up at the ceiling for days pondering the instructions on how to cut foam board to fit between the rafters. The yurt instructions stated this was sometimes necessary in "very cold" climates. Was that referring to Alaska or Maine? The idea of cutting sheets of foam in the yurt to wedge overhead sounded like an act of desperation to me. I hoped to leave such a feat as a worse case scenario. Heat rises to escape through the roof, but the ceiling fan had been reversed to push the heat back down. I really was hoping to avoid buying and cutting foam board.

Adam's solution was simple. Yes, heat would escape through the roof. But the most un-insulated part of the roof was the five-foot center dome. The polycarbonate kept in no heat. So Adam took the piece of liner fabric that had been cut at the factory to make the hole for the dome that had been included with the yurt (for patching material) and used it as a template to cut extra insulation that we'd used on the icebox. It was the same material used in the yurt walls and roof. He then pushed it above the ceiling fan and added some supports to keep it in place.

The effect was noticeable and not just in light blocked. There was a significant amount of heat retained, at least a five-degree difference. Losing the overhead light was a compromise I was willing to make to keep the added warmth. As the holidays closed in, we had three windows and the French doors letting in meager daylight, the stove roaring, and were maintaining a nice upper 60-degree temperature during the day. Nights still dropped down to the fifties inside. Whoever woke up and noticed the fire had died down received the honor of adding a few logs.

During this time, I overcame one thing about my yurt kitchen I found lacking. I loved cooking in the old house. If not meals, then cookies, or bread, something was always on the stove or in the oven. The yurt didn't have an oven. I had known my cooking habits and abilities would change with the yurt, so I'd entered the move to a small home very aware of new limitations. But I missed having an oven. Oven pancakes were one of my favorite breakfasts. Fresh zucchini bread, cinnamon rolls or a pound cake were small luxuries that no store bought variety could satisfy.

We still talked about a small 20-inch gas stove that was available from Premier. It was $500. But I was still feeling balky about that kind of money. We had only just begun to pay the yurt loan back. We still owed on the credit card. What we had worked, I just couldn't bake. Or at least that was what my mind was telling me. I took another look at my grill.

The grill in its summer glory

The grill was old and had three shelves under the barrel lid. It had a lot of room along with its two adjustable gas burners. Looking at it, I had to admit there wasn't much difference in concept between the grill as an oven and an oven. I wouldn't be able to tell the actual cooking temperature, so I'd have to pay close attention and go for an intuitive feel. But that was what had been done for centuries. I had to give it a try.

So one decent weekend day in December, not quite ready to finish shelf construction, I made a batch of zucchini bread and stuck it on the grill. An internet search had revealed a few grilled bread recipes, which gave me confidence. I checked it half a dozen times to be sure I wouldn't burn the bread. Finally, I stuck in a toothpick and it came out clean. The grill had worked. I savored my victory of warm zucchini bread along with a cup of hot tea. Oven pancakes were back on the menu.

It was nearly the holidays before the slush laden skies cleared for a full weekend. We had some snow on the ground, but not a full foot yet. The dreary weather and damp meant that bringing the saws up to the deck wasn't an option. Instead I made a dry space directly under the yurt next to the walls of the storage shed I'd built in the spring. There I began the process of measuring and cutting the remaining three shelf units for the kitchen.

Two sets of shelves were fairly straightforward. The most difficult part was that they ended just below the counter in the kitchen to leave room for the 16-gallon cistern and the 20-pound propane tank that fueled the on demand water heater and, with the magic of a connector hose and 'Y' valve, the two-burner stove as well. With only four shelves to build within the frame, construction went quickly. Hanging them was a bit more difficult as holding the heavy shelves in place while using the power drill to screw them into the frame was tricky. Sitting on the counter, I wedged a knee against a shelf to keep things stabilized. It worked and two more sets of shelves were quickly added to the kitchen.

About this time I'd come to the realization that if I'd built the frame of the wedge out of 2x12s, I could have just used the 1x12s I was using for shelves directly between the supports. Instead, I'd used 2x4s to save money on the front end and now had to make 1x12 boxes to support the internal shelves. What I was doing made attaching the shelves easier, as I could drill into them through the 1x12 sides thereby hiding the screws. And with the removal of the screws attaching the shelving units to the supports, I could take out the built-in shelves fairly quickly, in case we ever decided to take down the yurt and relocate. But the lack of foresight bothered me. I didn't get to decide which of the two options would be best.

The last set of shelves in the kitchen married the angled kitchen wall to the flat front. For this one I did screw in the 1x12 upright sides as there was no way to fit the wider back through the narrow front if I made the unit as one piece. I looked at the odd space to be filled with floor to ceiling shelves and pulled out a piece of cardboard. With pencil and scissors, I trimmed a template before heading outside to the brisk December afternoon to try a cut using both the miter and jigsaw.

To my surprise, the first shelf cut fit down to the little nub that overlapped the support board. With a quick success, I cut the remaining five matching pieces for floor, ceiling and three shelves. Feeling pretty good, I jumped ahead and cut the boards for the four "library" shelves on the side of the wedge opposite the kitchen. Before I called it quits for the day, I had two more sets of shelves built and installed. For Sunday, I had two straightforward sets of shelves, a tiny and bizarrely shaped nook bookcase, and a wish list item for Adam: a custom made ladder up to his comforter and pillow-lined loft.

The shelves opposite the kitchen and the ladder to the loft

With wood already cut, I got an early start in the morning. It was brisk and gray outside, not at all attractive for cutting wood under the deck where it remained dim until afternoon. If it hadn't been for the sawdust, I would have stayed in pajamas for a bit while screwing together the outside frames, marking where the shelves would go and then screwing the shelves in place. Far too quickly for such a cool morning, the last two easy shelves were in place.

The nook bookcase was going to be the home of our travel book collection, otherwise known as the "bad books" as they tended to inspire unorthodox ideas on what to do with our lives. We were very fond of them and couldn't wait to get the "bad book box" unpacked. The space was a tiny area made up of the angled side of the flat front's 2x12 header and footer beams with 2x4 supports on each side. With only eight inches of space for the 1x12 sides and shelves, I'd considered myriads of options to maximize room. In the end, I decided to use the same construction I had with all the bookcases, 1x12 frame with internal shelves. I measured and cut the side pieces, loosely set them in place and made a template for the tiny angled shelves.

Unlike the opposite shelf in the kitchen, the walls were parallel to each other, just with trapezoidal shelves between so that the front edges of the side supports were offset from each other by three inches. I planned to build this as a freestanding bookcase to be slid between the wedge supports. I took my template downstairs and jigged a first trial. No joy. Made a few adjustments. Almost there. A bit more smoothing and trimming. Finally, one worked. I made the matching seven shelves and assembled the unit.

It did not look like a bookcase. The unit resembled a Escher idea of a surreal and oddly proportioned shelf. Shrugging off the weird design, I slid it into place. It didn't fit. One support 2x4 that it had to slide against wasn't quite straight. There was no way to fix the beam, so the unit had to come apart and be recut. I took a break for lunch.

Trying again, I checked gaps and measurements, recutting all six shelves plus the top and bottom pieces. Back together again, the unit was still tight. The odd shape played with my sense of how it needed to fit. Wiggling it back and forth, the entire unit suddenly slid into place. I stood back, completely surprised and entirely pleased. My tiny nook bookcase fit and, now where it belonged, looked so cute and not at all out of place. Only one thing left to tackle.

The tiny and oh-so-difficult to construct "bad book nook"

For the ladder we had purchased nicely finished 2x6 pine. I had planned the six-inch overhang of the loft as a place to attach tap lights to shine onto my kitchen counter top, and because it gave us that bit of extra space for storage up top. Now I realized that the six-inch ladder supports fit into the overhang like I had designed it.

After days of building shelves, cutting the ladder rungs, figuring out the slight angle to make a steep ladder/staircase, and screwing the assembly together was a fairly simple process. By mid-afternoon, the ladder was slipped into the bottom of the overhang to rest against the lintel of the wedge. I gave a test climb. It was amazing how solid the wedge felt. With all the shelves adding stability, it didn't budge or wiggle. I sat amid the pillows and few odds and ends I'd managed to store around Adam's nest tired and happy. I had designed the wedge with its shelves, nooks, and loft. I had built it and it actually worked. Finally, I'd found the time and inclination to take on some woodworking. It had just taken me the sale of our house to do it.

Before I was completely done for the day, I took some scrap lumber and made two under- counter shelves to add storage to the kitchen side. After that as the early winter evening settled in with its bone chilling cold, I put away the few pieces of remaining lumber and stored the jig and saws in the "under-yurt" storage. I vowed that I was done constructing until spring. It was just too cold and raw to do more. Then I went into the yurt and took a long hot shower, grinning at my shelves the entire time.

I took pictures of the construction to send to my family to let them know what their present had become. Adam and I hadn't had a Christmas tree in years, finding the death of a small tree just to be decorated a few weeks with glass balls a sad event. We admired the tree over at Adam's parents', finding this year with the limited space an even better reason not to have a holiday tree. And living in Maine, we tended to be more excited about Winter Solstice anyway. From that point on we'd be gaining daylight once again. It was a nice consolation knowing the coldest months were still to come.

— Autumn

"It's flashy but I'll take this cold any day over that damn heat."

- Adam: 15 November 2010

Autumn is the woodworker of the family. She has the patience and the mathematical knowhow to cut the boards to the right length and correct angle. I've never been a fan of woodworking but am skilled in the other trades such as electrical and plumbing. It just makes sense. Take substance X and move it from point A to point B through a series of wires or pipes and make sure not to let any escape - very simple!

To hook up the shower inside required a few measurements, some drilling, and new wires run to an RV pump which moved the water from the rain barrel to the heat exchanger with plenty of pressure. The only issue was some pulsing, which I solved with a small pressure tank. In the end, while I did not like the wedge, I did appreciate the place to shower and the added storage. Yurts are not designed for storage.

Our little Morso created pleasant heat and made a beautiful sight!

With perspective and a much larger yurt community, I've now seen a yurt built on top of a standard garage. It is a brilliant idea. With storage, a place for a bathroom, and even a wood stove to take advantage of the additional heat rise, this option would solve so many problems we struggled with.

Heating a flashy yurt with nothing in the walls but fancy bubble wrap was a challenge. It consisted of removing drafts and insulating cold surfaces rather than holding heat like in a traditional house. We had already installed a nicely insulated floor and I had spent the fall gathering and stacking six cords of wood for the upcoming winter.

The yurt company we'd used sold window kits which were basically overpriced $200 pieces of reflecting bubble wrap that blocked out even more of our precious light; light that I needed to stay somewhat sane during our arctic and dark winter season. It led me to the conclusion to buy a roll of big bubble wrap at the local office supply and put several layers on the inside of the windows between the screen and the lattice. Fortunately it worked well. The only thing I did not insulate like this was the door. Being able to see outside from some vantage was important so we decided to leave the door clear.

— Adam

SNOWED UNDER
JANUARY & FEBRUARY 2011

"Today winter provided the yurt with one of nature's best forms of insulation: snow. Lots and lots of snow."

- Autumn:12 January 2011

Though we had a white Christmas, there was less than a foot of snow on the ground. We really didn't have much of the white stuff to deal with. The plummeting temperature was another issue altogether. Pacific Yurts sells winter insulation kits for the yurt's walls and windows. They sell the chimney kit for adding a wood stove safely and a snow load kit of heavy duty rafters with rafter supports to handle the extra weight on the roof. What they don't sell is an insulated top dome or weatherized door.

Insulating the top dome Adam had figured out in November by manufacturing an insert made of the same insulation used in the walls. The door was another issue. The French doors we had chosen were wooden with four panes to let in light. However the panes were plexiglass and only a single layer thick. The plexi had proven to have been a good idea as the door packaging had broken in shipment, rubbing the wood in a few places. If the windows had been glass, we would have been doorless until a replacement arrived. Not a situation we had wanted with only that one weekend to get the yurt assembled.

In the summer when we'd kept the door wide open and dropcloth screens over the opening to keep out bugs, the single pane plexiglass hadn't been an issue. As nighttime temperatures dipped below zero-degree Fahrenheit, the door became a cold abyss sucking out our valuable heat.

It was a coworker who came up with the perfect solution. She suggested we use the common Maine ingenuity of hanging a heavy duty blanket in front of the door. One weekend we were visiting the local hardware store and looked at hanging options. Not only did we find a beautiful rod with leaves tipping each end, we picked up metal rings with convenient alligator clips attached. Obviously we were not the first people who wanted to be able to hang something in front of an opening without a lot of sewing involved.

At home we found a heavy wool blanket and clipped it in. It was just wider than the door and covered it from floor to hanger. Bright red, it added a splash of color as we blocked out the night and cold beyond. I felt a link to the Mongolian nomads in their woolen gers and the tradition of hanging felted blankets to the walls to increase warmth. It really wasn't such a bad idea. And it worked.

The open door freezer effect was reduced. Mornings would come and we would pull back the blanket only to find the internal yurt condensation had collected and frozen on the icy door. The metal tread that ran to the outside air would be frozen to the door with a quarter inch of ice some mornings, requiring a bit of force to pull open the door.

With the blistering cold, keeping the fire going became an obsession. Though we meant to take turns in adding wood, my internal thermostat would wake me up an hour before Adam would have noticed the onset of cold as the fire died. Inevitably, I would be up three times a night on the worst nights to toss in a few logs. I preferred to keep the yurt in the fifties at night rather than let it drop lower and have that much more heat to gain once we woke up.

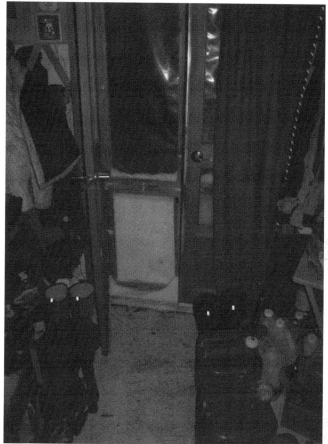

Yurt door with snow 1/3 way up Adam's storm doors made for the second winter – the red blanket is the door covering

We'd talked once about getting a propane heater to go against the wall, but we'd never decided on a size or where in our tiny and rather packed yurt to put it. And during the summer, it had been too hard to determine if we'd really need a propane heater. Saving our money had been an easier choice as we'd already bought the wood stove. For me, winter was quickly becoming a marathon of cold and little sleep.

The thin ice that formed on the lake in November and thickened during December was now freezing into a deep block. Ice shacks populated the lake into a makeshift nomadic village while trucks and snowmobiles traversed between on roads of frozen water. The first sound on weekend mornings would be ice augers drilling a new hole for fishing.

With all the natural refrigeration, using the antique icebox became a very simple affair. I would drop a set of blue freezer blocks onto the deck for a day or two. They would be frozen solid by the time the set in the freezer became slushy. There was no need for ice, but if there were we'd only need to look around the frozen ground. At least winter had made one thing easier. I started buying large gallons of milk and other produce I would have avoided holding onto for more than one day in the summer such as fish. Our food selection flourished.

The first major storm hit January 11th to 12th. Over a foot and a half of snow fell in soft petals of cold. We watched the world settle under the layer of snow from the warm refuge of our yurt. The biggest entertainment beyond watching the inches pile up was the traffic on the main road between us and the lake. Monitoring plows and the speed of vehicles gave us regular road condition updates. It didn't look good out there. Speed demons on the curvy lakeside road fell down to a mere crawl. Plows ran by every half hour, their scraping blade along the asphalt audible when they were a mile off. Lines of traffic grew behind each flashing plow that would shepherd the cars safely along roadways. I was happy to be snowed in and not on the road.

Mini-avalanches fell from the yurt roof as the snow piled up. The shed mass formed a shell against the yurt up to the windows. Between the frequency of plows on the road and avalanche rates from the yurt roof, I could gauge how the storm progressed all night without the need to open my eyes.

When I woke the morning of the 12th, I was first surprised at how warm the yurt felt. The inevitable morning chill was noticeably absent. I checked the outdoor temperature on the weather station: -5 degrees Fahrenheit. That was normal. Then I realized what was going on – snow.

Inuit people had long ago figured out that snow is a great insulator. Igloos hold warmth. A round yurt covered in snow is not much different in concept. We had just gained over a foot of new insulation on the outside of the yurt. I began to love winter.

The yurt weathering a snow storm

Adam shoveled the deck, adding a few more inches to the snow pile at the yurt's base. After that, he used snowshoes to stomp paths to the car, his parents' house, and the outhouse. The idea of putting on a coat and knee-high muck boots to head out to the bathroom oddly didn't bother me. Once the path was made through the woods, I found I enjoyed heading outdoors into the snow and under naturally decorated pines. Until Adam whacked me with a snowball as I walked back. At least there was plenty of ammo to return fire.

Water remained an odd situation. We would get drinking water by filling one gallon jugs from either my office or Adam's folks' house. Water for the shower cistern was harder to come by. During the summer, we could have drilled a well and installed a frost free pump. It hadn't been due to the cost that it had never been discussed, though a well in Maine can easily run $5,000 and be over 200 feet deep. For me a well would have meant we were settled.

Where the yurt sat worked. We had a great view of the lake and a spot for gardens. It had been an unused, shrubby patch of untended yard before we moved in. But it was less than 2,000 feet away from Adam's parents' 150-year-old colonial. While I appreciated the land and the chance to figure out how to live in a yurt on solar power, I couldn't say I felt this was where we were going to stay. The yurt could be taken down and moved. A well could not. It might have been a logical decision, but it left us in a water lurch.

We found two options for finding water to fill the cistern. Neither was fun. One of the heavy duty plastic bins we'd used to pack our belongings from the old house was placed next to the door. Adam filled the bin the first time by using the Coleman five- and seven-gallon water jugs filled from his parents' house. After that, we added snow.

There was plenty of snow and the bin was next to the door. We'd use a large pot and my canner to scoop up snow and drop it in the bin before we went to bed. The next night, the snow would be melted. We'd use the water to fill the cistern after taking a shower and then drop in more snow until the bin was filled.

This worked except that the snow had less water content than the same volume of water. Over the course of the week, we'd have a net loss in water in the bin. Plus unless it snowed, we'd be going further from the door to bring in more snow. Going out to shovel snow into pots after a warm shower simply wasn't fun.

The alternative was melting snow on the weekends. We'd put the canner and a massive pasta pot full of snow onto the wood stove early in the morning. We rarely ventured out for errands on the weekends, finding them easier to do after work when we were already in town. So by the end of the day we could manufacture four to six pots of water. It was usually enough to fill up the bin and the cistern to start a new week.

The cistern was its own headache. It was only 16 gallons. We'd planned on buying a second so that we'd have a larger supply of water. After seeing how difficult it was to keep a 16-gallon cistern full, we didn't want to have a larger one for the winter. We had to fill the 16-gallon one nightly if we didn't want to spend an hour or so filling it every three days. I calculated that we used around three and a half gallons of water for showers between the two of us. We tried to use less, but that was the average. It meant that the 16 gallons were only good for four days if we were careful and could suck the cistern dry.

To fill it, I'd made the bottom shelf in the kitchen pop out. We could then use a large funnel to fill the cistern from the kitchen side of the wedge, which was closer to the door and bin. It had sounded practical when designed, but in use was difficult. Water tended to drip as it was being poured, splashing across the counter. The dishes needed to be out of the way, so they had needed to be done before we filled the cistern. Filling it became a headache accomplished just before bed when we were tired. It wasn't the best arrangement even if it worked. We were looking forward to a break.

The first two weeks of February were to be a vacation to the shores of Spain. We were nervous about leaving the yurt cold, but we were excited at the idea of unlimited hot showers and a break from the constant feeding of the stove. We started preparing the yurt for its deep freeze in mid-January. We brought up two empty bins and as we found things that should not be frozen, dropped them in to be taken to Adam's parents' for storage.

The weekend of January 29th, we stopped filling the cistern. We wanted it drained before we left for an overnight hotel at the airport on the 31st. Our flights would take us to sunny Spain on February 1st. With a giddy sense of getting away without completing our chores, we took longer showers and went to bed without the rigamarole of water responsibilities.

The biggest storm of the year hit overnight from January 30th to 31st. Nearly two feet of snow fell and a second smaller storm was nudging in behind to hit New England on February 2nd to 3rd. If our flights didn't get out on time, we would be stuck in Maine until at least the weekend losing our first week of vacation.

Before we could even see if the bus was still running to Boston, Adam got the notice that our flights were cancelled. This was to have been our first vacation with my mother-in-law. Adam slogged through the three feet of snow on the ground to tell her the news. When he came back, he told me the rest of it.

"The whole trip is cancelled."

Losing the first week and problems with rescheduling hotels in foreign countries much less the airlines being inundated with a re-booking nightmare of a Nor'Easter with its twin coming in behind, the entire vacation fell apart. Disappointment was cast aside in a building panic as we realized we had no water. Even the storage bin next to the door had been drained as well as the drinking water.

It took the rest of the snow-filled day to restore all the yurt systems and bring back our bins of items not to be frozen. As another night fell, we were settled again but feeling out of sorts. We were supposed to have been in Boston that night. Our luggage of warmer weather clothing sat abandoned on the yurt floor. It would take me a week and through the second Nor'Easter until I finally decided I wanted the square footage that the luggage occupied enough to face unpacking.

Snow fireworks off the yurt deck – all you need is VERY cold temperatures and a cup of boiling water tossed skyward

To add to our winter woes, our solar system started to read a yellow warning for days on end. When at least 85% charged, a small light would indicate green. Below that we would have yellow. We never wanted to see red. If a red light started flashing, it was time to buy new batteries.

A friend familiar with solar power had told me over the summer that batteries wanted to be at the same temperature we were. They would last the longest and hold the best charge if kept at 60 to 70 degrees. We'd put ours in an unheated room under the yurt.

Adam assured me the water in the batteries wouldn't freeze as long as they stayed charged. Now our indicator was saying that our use was greater than the sunshine. The batteries were not fully charged. With layers of clouds and storm after storm, the batteries were not likely to have a substantial amount of sun for some time. We did our best to limit electricity usage.

Adam had wired a plug-in floor lamp to the more efficient DC power. I used it in the kitchen when cooking or doing dishes. Now I did my best to rely first on the LED tap lights. It meant I went through AAA batteries fairly quickly, but that was better than draining the deep cycle batteries tied to the solar panel. There wasn't much we could do about the water pump to the shower, but I could reduce the drain caused by recharging my laptop. I took it to work and plugged it in there. Movies or documentaries on the flat screen were limited to a few times a week.

The weather was also taking its toll on the grill. It was a hybrid of two similar grills and the oldest pieces were going on fifteen years, the newest were hard to find replacements of less than a year. With my discovery that the grill worked as an outdoor oven, I'd begun to use it heavily. Whether it was the cold or ice build-up, I wasn't sure, but one of the two knobs controlling the flow of gas began to stick. Sometimes it would not turn on, sometimes it wouldn't turn off unless extreme force was used.

First I began to only use both burners when necessary, then I got Adam to look at it. He found corrosion and wear on the internal parts. He fixed the first valve, but by the end of February the second was starting to show the same symptoms. He agreed he'd fix it if it got to that point but pointed out what I didn't want to hear. The grill was dying. I would soon be without an oven again.

Coworkers and family kept asking how the yurt was holding up with the winter. "Is it warm enough?" was a much asked question. There was no denying I was tired. Putting wood in the stove two or more times a night was wearing. The water situation wasn't fun even if we were getting by. I really had no good answer. The rare days the sun was out, the yurt would keep a nice 70-plus during the day with the stove barely going, especially with snow around the walls up to the windows. But when cold, clear nights set in, it was cold.

Then Adam's dad came over to ask us something. "It's warm in here, warmer than the house," he said as he headed back out. It gave me pause. The yurt was warmer than his traditional, if 150-year old, house with its pellet stoves and furnace? Snapped out of the reality of long nights and difficulties, I could compare this winter to previous ones. He was right. The yurt was warmer.

Our old cape had been 200 years old. A timber frame sitting atop a dirt floor, fieldstone foundation, it had always been drafty. The yurt walls moved in the wind and sometimes delivered a puff of cool air. But the yurt had nowhere near the draftiness or cold spots of that old house. There had been times when I described the insulation in the walls of the house as feeling like they had dissolved. I assumed that it was simply because the 'R' value of the insulation had been surpassed. It had felt like we were living with nothing more than plywood between us and winter. The only warm spot had been two feet from the fire, day or night.

The yurt wasn't that bad. On cold nights equal to those that would send the house into deep freeze, we were holding above fifty. During the day, we were toasty and in the sixties to seventies. There were never days of two pairs of socks, floors too cold to walk on, sweaters worn while sitting under covers on the warm side of the couch. The yurt was really not that bad. Someone with a modern and well wrapped house might have had a different view of the spectrum, but that wasn't where we were coming from. For us the yurt was an improvement.

The end of February finally brought us a trip away from the yurt. It wasn't to a warmer clime, but it was to a bed and breakfast in Ottawa with free hot tea on order and plenty of hot water in the shower. A potential life alternative necessitated a trip to the Canadian capitol for two nights. A storm that came through on Friday the 25th extended our stay a third.

The first night at the bed and breakfast, we happily took turns for marathon showers. A few minutes into mine, I was bored. Then I started to feel bad about all the water I was using. What on earth did I used to do in the shower that took ten minutes? I stood under the admittedly lovely rain of steaming water and then stuck my head out.

"Do you want your turn now?"

Adam looked over at me. "For goodness sakes, just enjoy it while you can." I laughed and went back to my shower. He was right. I only had three nights of unlimited hot water and tea I didn't have to brew myself. I was just going to have to find a way to make the best of it.

— Autumn

> *"Damn deck!! I sure hope it holds up under all this snow. Worst mistake ever hiring a couple locals with no more carpentry knowledge than which way to hold a hammer!"*
>
> \- Adam: 20 January 2011

Winter in Maine is a challenge. The snow is heavy, the air damp, and, if not damp, then cold as hell. We get ice storms, major wind, a hundred different types of snow, and let's not even get into the nasty cold spell that settles on the state in January. It makes December cold look like beach weather. Maine is not a warm state, but it is warm enough for road salt to work ... on rusting our cars away. The salt also is spread by big, noisy trucks which cast rumbling sounds up to our amplifying yurt.

In addition to the plows, snow created an interesting experience. Let's say we never actually used our snow load kit. Every snowstorm would fall on the yurt. Slowly you would hear cracking. The entire yurt shook as a roof load of snow fell at once. Our dog at the time was just a puppy and developed a roof noise complex that exists to this day.

The fallen snow helped insulate the yurt. But keeping the yurt insulated with snow had challenges. The heat from inside would melt the snow against the walls, reducing the natural insulation by several inches. Each night I would go out and re-shovel snow against the walls, filling in the gap.

Water and electricity remained a challenge as well. As much as we wished to remain off "shore" power, we had to keep an extension cord available. Water was often gathered in five-gallon containers hauled on a sled from my parents' spigot. Melting snow was common. We quickly learned ice was the best thing to melt as it had the highest water content.

The electricity issue was always in the forefront of my mind. We never had enough juice, always too little. We would hit 11.6 volts on the display and that would be our cutoff for all use that evening. I had wired a switch to kill the inverter to prevent complete battery drainage. If that happened, the risk of destroying our cold stored batteries would be imminent. In one bad stretch, we actually hooked a car battery charger to our battery bank to bring up the power level ... the sun was not enough for our four batteries and 205-watt solar panel.

The plumbing remained an ongoing struggle. As we discovered one night when the hot water heater didn't have enough flow to start. It took some frustrated troubleshooting to solve what was wrong. I had installed two hose filters on our water feed that the pump drew from for showers. Through the course of operation, these filters became dreadfully clogged by detritus - from the snow. Snow is actually not at all clean. Towards the end, we decided it was best to simply filter the snow water before filling the cistern to reduce the times we had to clean the hose filters. Adapt or be dirty!

We also learned one thing you do NOT do when living in a sub-freezing climate in a yurt is actually try to go on a trip. IT DOES NOT WORK. Living in a yurt during the winter is a task for hands-on people. You must keep the fire fed, the snow shoveled, and the tea warm. There is no room for a trip to Spain or Ottawa. If you do, plants die and things that should not freeze do.

A calm winter day with chimney smoking

This was the case upon the return from our trip to Ottawa. It turns out that our hot water heater, while it did have a freeze safe drain, it did not have a snow detritus filter. And that compromised it. During our absence, the water in the manifold froze and created a beautiful water-gushing crack. Having little money, I took it upon myself to open up the heater and try my hand at brazing which surprisingly worked very well, allowing us to use the heater again.

Mount Crapper: In the summer when things are growing and the ecosystem functions matter decays. In the winter it slows and almost stops. The same principles apply when it comes to an unheated outhouse. We did not build a very deep pit in the outhouse, only about two feet. In the summer this was fine as the added organics broke down well. In the winter, however, it just piled and by mid winter it was getting dangerously close to the deposit hatch. The task fell to me to solve this problem, and, fortunately, frozen waste tends to fall over. A stick was dedicated as the crap poker. Two to three times that year, the poker was put into action. Lesson learned ... build an appropriately sized chamber beneath the outhouse.

— Adam

THINKING SPRING
MARCH & APRIL 2011

"For the last five or so years every time we've left Maine, I haven't been happy to come back. It told me it was time for a change, but every time I looked at new jobs the switch in state didn't feel like a good choice. I felt stuck. But this time when we came back from the cruise, it was the first time in years that I was happy to come home."

- Autumn: 8 April 2011

We still had a deep snow pack of over two feet as March arrived in Maine. The longer days and greater period of calm between storms began to show in our solar charging. The battery indicator began to read green again a few times a week. Along with solar gain, March brought a financial turning point as well.

Adam and I have always been early tax filers, mainly due to the fact that we overpay our taxes and receive a healthy refund. I've had tax accountants tell us how silly this was. That was our money we were sending bi-weekly to the federal government to hold until the new year. Instead, we should budget better and put that money in a savings account to earn interest for us. A great idea, but another one that sounded better on paper than was worth the implementation.

To budget so precisely would take some trial and error. I really didn't want to err too badly and owe money. And though we had been free from credit card debt before purchasing the yurt, we still tended to gobble up money in the bank account. I had dreams of having a savings account under my control and did keep a buffer to cover the checking account, but for now the federally forced savings account brought about by overpaying my taxes worked.

As the state and federal refunds came into our bank, we paid down the credit card at long last. We also paid off a healthy amount on the yurt construction loan. Including the monthly payments I'd been making since fall, we had the yurt and deck half paid off with our first spring on the horizon.

In my most optimistic dreams, I'd wanted the yurt loan paid off in the first year. Despite not meeting that goal, I wasn't unhappy knowing we should be able to pay it off within one more year. The idea of owning where I lived and not having a mortgage payment made an alluring goal. It had been one of the reasons I'd agreed to selling the house and moving into the yurt. We were halfway there.

The spring freezing and thawing pushed the old grill to its aged limits. The second gas knob became unusable and I began avoiding the grill as much as possible. Adam and I looked for other options. We considered a ship's oven and range. It was the perfect size, smaller than the 20-inch Premier gas stove we'd looked at before buying the yurt - one that I now realized would be deeper and higher than my counter tops and so block some of my newly built shelves. Boat stoves were ruled out before we got beyond the "oh, that would work!" stage. The cost for the average model was over $1,000. I began to give up on ovens.

I don't know how Adam stumbled across it, but one day he sent me a link to an outdoor oven by Camp Chef. The self-igniting propane oven could fit a lasagna pan. It had a two burner range on top, both self-igniting as well. The downside was the small BTU output. The benefit was that it only cost $200 and could be run on mini-cylinders or a 20-pound tank.

The Camp Chef arrived on March 7th. The drop down cover that fastened over the range and the instructions were full of dire warnings about using the oven indoors. It could produce carbon monoxide. The last time either Adam or I had checked, burning anything with open flame produced carbon monoxide. A well made stove would produce a minimal amount. In either case we weren't overly worried, the yurt was hardly air tight.

The new Camp Chef stove

The biggest hurdle to indoor installation that Adam found was the lack of a heat shield. That could be an issue, especially with the shower cistern directly behind part of where the oven would be located. I made a template out of cardboard. Adam took it down to the shed where he cut and bent a piece of sheet metal. The heat shield was ready by March 11th.

With a snow pack around the yurt, I was back to cutting wood under the deck once again. I pulled apart my kitchen counter top one final time and started rearranging. I built a small shelf cabinet for the new oven to sit on and put tiles on top to handle any excess heat. I'd measured the stove's final height to be above the counter by half an inch. Due to the propane hook-up in the back, the stove had to sit to the left of a support beam for the wedge frame. It couldn't go any further to the right or the metal legs to the old workbench would no longer fit.

The metal legs of the old workbench were barely noticeable and hardly took up any room. Plus they could handle quite a bit of weight, so I wanted to keep using them as my main counter support. It didn't give me much wiggle room for the new oven as I needed to maintain a spot to the left of it for the wash basin as that was where the drinking water ceramic crock was located on the shelves. And it was the only spot that would fit the crock's height and weight.

The kitchen area before the Camp Chef oven

I maneuvered the workbench into place and checked the measurement for my new counter top. I'd bought a piece of pine board that was 18" wide and made of numerous joined sections. It looked like butcher's block but was only one-inch deep. It meant I needed to add boards to match the height of the old counter, which is the dimension I'd used when I built the in-wall kitchen shelves.

I also had to notch the new counter top to fit on either side of a rafter support for the yurt. It took some measuring and some jigging, but I finally had my new counter top in place. With a trip board underneath it, it even looked like a traditional counter top. I was feeling quite proud.

For the left side of the stove, I utilized one of the once under-counter storage units I'd made with scrap lumber in December. With some modification, I fit the remaining length of counter board to the top and slid it into place. The construction hadn't taken a full day and I had installed my new oven/range top and new counters. Except for a jelly cabinet that took up too much space in my eyes, my kitchen was done. The next morning, I made popovers in the oven, enjoying the fact that I could watch my breakfast cook in the comfort of my kitchen.

The kitchen after the Camp Chef installation

The most difficult part of the new oven was that it was not thermostatically controlled. Instead, you turned the oven on full, brought it to temperature as indicated by a temperature gauge, and then tried to maintain the proper temperature by turning the gas down or opening the door if necessary, which usually resulted in turning the temperature back up. Reviews online had been mixed on this feature. After cooking outside on a grill that also lacked a thermostat control and no temperature gauge at all, operating the new oven was a breeze.

By the end of the following week, the snow had melted. The lakes remained frozen, but that Sunday we passed the Equinox and spring came officially to Maine. Finally with days and nights of equal length and the winter blanket of thick clouds behind us, the solar panel had sufficient light to charge fully. It was one more worry behind us, but one we'd have to think about before the next winter arrived.

With warmer temperatures, we began to remove insulation from the windows and top dome the week before we headed to Puerto Rico to meet up with my parents for a cruise. Minimal living and being self sufficient had become ingrained to our psyches by this point. Adam and I each only packed one travel backpack for the week long cruise which included a few days in Puerto Rico at either end. We also bunked the night before the cruise on the floor of my parents' hotel room to save money.

Actually, the plan was to bunk on their floor, but we found out they were on the ground floor and had a patio which connected to the hotel pool area. We slept outside, Adam on a few cushions while I had an air mattress provided by the hotel. By midnight, the air mattress was flat and I wandered poolside and scrounged a few damp but comfortable cushions for myself. It felt nomadic to be unencumbered but comfortable with our mere backpacks of belongings.

On the cruise, we made thorough use of the shower in our room, washed our clothing in the sink, and made a point not to spend any money on the ship. Drinking water was provided in our room for a fee. We went up a couple of floors and filled our hydro packs at the water fountains next to the food courts. The only paid excursion we took was on the last day to leave the ship and see my parents off at the airport. Otherwise, we navigated around the islands by bus, taxi, and walking. We had a grand time.

It took me weeks to realize our independence on the cruise stemmed partially from our life in the yurt. We were used to figuring things out for ourselves. To have everything catered so that not one moment of the day brought a difficulty was artificial to us. Half the adventure was figuring it out for ourselves. It made us appreciate every sight, every swim in the ocean, and every well earned beer. Just like every success with overcoming a challenge in the yurt. We no longer considered the obstacles that cropped up as problems. They were just difficulties we hadn't found the solution to yet.

Coming home to Maine, even with the lakes still frozen, was a good feeling. It was the first time in ages that I was happy to be back. For years, I'd dreaded returning to my life after a vacation. Even in Puerto Rico there had been a moment of "oh if only we could get a plane to Central America." With a backpack of essentials, I was ready to wander the world. Except that I missed our two dogs. And I really didn't mind the yurt. I no longer wanted to change every aspect of my life, just a marginalized portion. I could see it wasn't Maine I didn't like or how I lived my life, but how much time I had to spend away from home at work. Finally, I knew the source of my unhappiness and had a problem I could focus on fixing.

We hadn't "winterized" the yurt before leaving for the cruise. Days were above freezing, especially sunny ones in the yurt. Nights could dip low, but not so low that we thought we had to worry about something freezing in the few hours it was cold. For the most part that was true.

A bit of water I'd left in the dog's water bowl was a frozen lump. All else appeared well until Adam checked out the bathroom. Water had frozen in the plumbing leading to the instant water heater. One valve was broken, which Adam managed to bypass. It was a reminder not to take for granted the spring conditions of Maine or what hazards were possible when living in a giant tent.

Returning to the silence that is spring in Maine, we listened to the world reawaken. Geese came north though the lakes only had small patches of open water even though it was early April. On warm evenings, woodcock and peepers would sound off. The coyotes howled on the ridge. Finally during a windy spring rain, the ice on the lake broke. Water once again reflected the blue sky bordered by pines and trees breaking bud.

Warm temperatures meant that I could no longer freeze ice blocks on the deck. The blue blocks returned to the freezer we'd kept in Adam's parents' garage. Adam frowned at the idea of using the antique icebox all summer again. But a new solution hadn't formed for either of us yet, so I began the ritual of swapping out ice and frozen blocks. At least so early in the season, the ice would last three or four days.

We no longer needed to burn the wood stove during the day. Instead we loaded wood in the morning and then dampened the stove fully. By the cool of evening, there were still sufficient embers to light a small fire. The nights were warm enough that I no longer woke to load the stove. Spring was a gentle season even when rain pounded the yurt overnight. By morning, the world smelled like fresh earth as the grass turned green and the oak saplings around our deck opened leaves.

By the end of April, all of the winter insulation was off the yurt. We even opened the windows and top dome during the warmest hours of the day. Spring air flooded our little home. The two awnings were installed and we debated buying two or three more for the remaining windows. They were a great protection from rain.

Adam mentioned selling the composting toilet and I agreed. The outhouse had functioned all winter. With a few bins of possessions still without a home in the small yurt, I was open to keeping the toilet facilities out of the yurt for both space and worry on smell as well as privacy. He and I saw each other constantly in the yurt. Going to another place for a few minutes of privacy to take care of some needed business had its benefits, even if it was raining out.

With the warmth, we switched our shower water source back to the outside 55-gallon rain barrel. Though we still did not have gutters to capture water off the yurt, we overcame our need for self sufficiency enough to run a hose once a week from Adam's parents' house. Once again, we could take slightly longer showers without having to pay for it in time spent refilling the inside cistern. With the oven, outside water barrel, and moderate temperatures the biggest difficulties were remembering to put new ice blocks in the freezer and making sure we didn't run out of propane. Life felt easy again.

—Autumn

"Another year survived, I finally get my bright and airy yurt back."

- Adam: 20 March 2011

M aine is known for several seasons: fall when the fairs occur, hunting season when the gun shots happen but nothing dies, winter when people are enjoying the snow, more winter when people are putting hits out on the weatherman and the police are scrambling to provide protection, tourney time when all the crazed Mainers with cabin fever go nuts over high school basketball, mud season when many cars vanish in the potholes, construction season where you spend more time looking at a stop sign held by a guy who won't look directly at you and there is no visible construction by the time you get through, and, finally, a few days of the rare summer season before fall hits again. Out of all of them I enjoy fall the best, but in the yurt mud season, otherwise known as spring for those from away, is a close second.

Spring is a time for catching up on sleep, growing plants, repairing those things that needed help but couldn't be practically fixed in the winter. It is a time to dry and air things out. The yurt really needed both.

The yurt in spring

Daily I hauled as much as was feasible outside. The large carpet that sat between the wedge and futon and, thankfully, hid our rough floor was hung over the deck rail. After a few days, I replaced it with extra blankets that we no longer needed nightly. Anything I could find and move went for a turn outside in the sun. The constant rearranging and cleaning not only freshened the yurt, but helped de-clutter the small space. I left a few items outside as our living space grew to include the deck.

The Composting Toilet Saga: With the decision made to sell the toilet, I listed it in the local want ads, craigslist, and on ebay. We received several offers, including a generous Nigerian guy who wanted to pay us an extra $50,000 dollars for it but did not want to help with the shipping logistics and a hardship case that wanted us to donate the toilet to her as she was broke and needed help. In the end we received a proper offer from a nice lady in the southeast who not only wished to buy it, but took care of all the shipping issues. I just needed to drop it off at the UPS store, clean and ready for them to box up.

There are two specific viewpoints of a clean composting toilet. One is "new" clean. The other is "spending the year under the yurt deck but unused" clean. Ours was the latter. I drained the rainwater that had accumulated, removed leaf debris from the inside, wiped it down, and plopped it in the jeep to head to the UPS center.

I showed up and the three employees looked at me apprehensively when I told them I had the toilet ready to go. They hesitantly asked, "is it clean?" "Of course," I answered. "I took care of that this morning."

We all looked down the honey shoot to confirm my statement and they gasped. Apparently I missed one stubborn squirrel nest and a couple of pine cones. I said oops, and, without hesitation, reached my hand down to grab the pine cones and leaves, causing one employee to leave the room. I asked where I could toss them and the manager stood stunned, unable to answer at first. She finally whispered "the dumpster." They eventually took the toilet, and I could not have gotten out of there quicker. I suspect that was the first AND last toilet shipment they took!

— Adam

FINDING HOME
MAY 2011

"I had to ask myself if I could live anywhere and in any way, what would I choose? The answer surprised me. It shows me we still have work to do, but we are on the right track."

            - Autumn: 6 May 2011

M ay came with green fullness and for me, a cold. Staying home to sleep off a fever, I had an odd dream. It was of a hard sided yurt.

Yurts come in two categories, though most websites label three. There are yurts like the one we bought with a lattice framework covered with fabric walls and roof. This is a soft sided yurt. It breathes with the wind. Some companies sell modifications to install a section to hold a traditional window. Otherwise, the only full opening to the outside is through the door. The windows have sewn in screens and the top dome opens a mere three inches.

Next are hard sided yurts. Made of wooden or plywood walls, this category has been broken down into two types: tapered wall and modular. The modular yurt is formed by short sections of straight wall that can be bolted together. It is still an impermanent structure since the panels can be taken down, stacked, and shipped elsewhere.

The tapered wall yurt is something different. A cross between a soft sided yurt that depends on a cable to lend support to the wall/rafter interface, its sides are made out of wood angled outward to rest on the cable. Aesthetically, I find this yurt the most beautiful with its curves and angles. Usually constructed with a full circle of windows, if not two layers of them, they are light and airy.

My feverish dream was of a tapered wall yurt full of glass and light. It was steel, glass, and wood. Interior walls were short sections of frosted panes on central pivots, allowing both openness or privacy when needed. I woke and drew out my dream, knowing what I'd seen was too expensive to build. But I wanted to capture a place that felt safe to me, flooded with inspiration and peace. Even if it would only exist as a sanctuary in my mind, sketching the lines etched it firmly into my consciousness. I did not want to forget.

It was a few days later as I looked over the details I saw some similarities to another house design I'd once liked. Years before when Adam had learned of my love for log cabins and timber frame homes, he'd ordered catalogues on house designs. Among them had come one for an octagon log cabin. I'd fallen in love with the central kitchen that looked out to a window filled living room. A hallway wrapped around the central room leading to the bedrooms.

Thinking about it now, I recognized the design for what it was: a hard sided yurt. Connections began to link in my mind. The October before we sold the house, Adam and I along with my parents had gone to Costa Rica. We'd visited a resort deep in the rainforest constructed with a safari theme. The rooms had actually been large Livingstone style tents with a back addition for a high end bathroom. We'd all been rather charmed with the resort, my parents included. Just over a year later, I was living in a very large tent.

Yurt dreams peppered May, only I did not realize they were yurt dreams. They confused me at first. I kept dreaming Adam and I lived out in the open, but we were happy. We would be snug in a clearing in the forest with our furniture scattered about: the fridge, the futon, a kitchen space. Often right before I woke up, I'd ask myself how we could be so happy since I didn't see any protection from the rain. It didn't make any sense to me, but it was a dream.

It was after the second content-living-outside dream that I finally realized what was going on. The clearing in the woods was how my subconscious interpreted the yurt. We could hear the outdoors so well through our walls and we spent so much time outside, that in the deepest part of my mind it was as if there were no walls at all.

A typical view of the interior of our real yurt

I wondered about this sudden yurt fixation. We were at almost a full year living in our little yurt. I thought that might be the root of the dreams and revelations. A year was something to mark as an event, a time to really prove whether it was possible or not to live in a yurt in Maine. It made sense that yurts were on my mind. I'm introspective by nature.

But the one-year marker did not explain the hard sided yurt dream or why it lingered so much in my consciousness. Whenever I was stressed at work, I started thinking about my dream yurt. I tried to figure out the architectural details. It had a staggered level floor to offset different living areas and to fit the rocky ledge on which it perched. My mind dove into how the yurt would function, its eclectic intricacies, and its peaceful light. The dream became my month-long obsession.

Meanwhile, my real yurt needed a spring cleaning. Without the wood stove going, it was time to clean the yurt from top to bottom. The bin where I kept my spring clothes was brought up from the under-yurt storage. Winter sweaters and coats were swapped for shorts and short sleeved shirts. The floor Adam had painted a sandy taupe had not held up well over the winter, showing stains. We debated whether to repaint or replace.

With the multiple intrusions made by the rafter supports plus the screws and plates anchoring each to the floor, I could not imagine putting down a hardwood floor. Yet that was what I had wanted. We thought about installing flooring except for the outer circle between the rafters, where maybe we could lay a board to fit the awkward space between rafters. But then we'd also have to deal with how the lattice touches the floor twice between each set of rafter supports. The technicalities were complicated. It would have been better to install a nice floor before we put up the yurt. Of course, the torrential rain the weekend we had erected the yurt would not have been very good for the floor.

An inside view looking the other way

It was a roundabout conversation without a decision. Painting would work, but would have to be done in sections and would smell. And it wouldn't remove the dirt trapping pattern of the plywood surface. We were living with an under-floor that had been made into the main floor. It worked but was hard to keep clean and wasn't pretty. I tried to settle with accepting it.

Early spring is a sweet time in Maine. The weather is often warm enough to be outside during the day, and the biting insects haven't hatched yet. Cruelly right around Mother's Day, the black flies usually emerge. Just when having the doors wide open to catch the spring air was the most enjoyable, we had to start dropping the screen cloth over the door once again.

Consisting of screening material made in two pieces wider than the door, they didn't fully cover the opening. Even the summer before there had always been gaps to let in a handful of clever bugs. I tried various methods of securing the fabric, but anything that worked was quickly dislodged when one of us had to go out.

Having the screens down made me think of summer and the impending heat. The idea of the heavy air felt suffocating. It was only May and I was getting anxious about July. Another year of heat, the antique icebox running too warm, and biting insects that emerged at dusk when it was cool. I was tired and out of inspiration. But I kept having dreams of living happily in my wall-less forest.

One quiet day mid-May I finally sat down and asked myself, if I could live anywhere and in any way, how would I live. I thought not just of countries but of ways of living from practical to impractical. A hut in the rainforest? A mansion in England? Our old house? A newly made version of our old house? Where would I be happy and feel the contentedness that infused my dreams?

I had asked a lot of my coworkers who had been in shock to learn I was selling my house to move into a giant tent: "What was the harm in giving it a try?" Yurts hold their value. We found after some research that they are in fairly high demand even in Maine. Used for everything from recreational huts to dwellings, I knew several people who had owned one while building bigger homes. Now I faced what I wanted to do with my yurt. Was this my permanent home or just a step to something else?

After thinking of and rejecting idea after idea, I finally thought of a living situation that instantly clicked. If I could live anywhere, it would be in the forest. Preferably a mixed deciduous forest as I felt a strong connection to its seasonality and structure. If I could live in anything, it would be something small. I like doing without.

I want just the basics so that I'm not distracted from the world outside. The two houses I'd owned had felt natural with wooden trim and cabinets, but they'd always contrived to keep me indoors rather than out. The yurt was the first time I'd spent every moment I could on the deck. And I really liked the round shape. It was harmonious. It said I'm different with a soft shout. A little log cabin would do, but a yurt with its lofty ceiling and light from all sides felt spacious both physically and mentally.

It was that moment when I realized that I chose to live like this. Given all the options, there were a few things I'd change. A few things could be made easier. I'd rather be in the forest, not have it a few feet from the yurt. I'd love to have a stream nearby. I'd like easy access to a water supply.

The outhouse didn't bother me. Not having cable or any TV hadn't bothered me for years. I felt I owned too many clothes but hadn't figured out how to make less work with my job. I liked my kitchen. I liked my oven quite a lot. I liked that if I didn't like something, I could change it. This was not a $20,000 kitchen with expensive cabinets. If I wanted a change, I was out a couple hundred dollars and some time. Any improvement I could think of, Adam or I could find a way to manufacture. Living in a yurt was empowering.

With the realization that I liked the yurt, the annoyances that had built up through the spring faded away. The yurt wasn't perfect, but it was a better lifestyle than the old house. I was happier. I felt I got more from life, experienced it more, and was closer to the things that mattered.

In town, our local food cooperative began to put out the spring seedlings. The last frost in Maine can occur anytime between mid-May to early June. It was still a little early to plant unless I wanted to fashion row covers. I wasn't quite up to that yet, but it was time to get the raised beds ready.

I cleaned out any stalks buried under snow the fall before. Adam and I purchased lobster compost to add to the top of the beds. I raked it in as we began to debate what to fit into our small garden.

"I think we should get those Belgian hot peppers again," I told Adam.

"I can't believe you want to plant hot peppers. You hate hot peppers."

"Jalapeños," I argued. "And eggplants. I want to grow eggplants again."

The list grew larger than the three raised beds. We kept an eye on the weather as well as seedling sales.

— Autumn

"Sometimes I wonder if I'm the crazy one."

\- Adam: 15 May 2011

W hen I decided on the yurt, I weighed it between a live-aboard boat, a container house, or a tiny home. I convinced Autumn on the idea of a yurt. Needless to say it proved an interesting experience. I could not believe she now wanted to build a hard sided one.

A local eccentric by the name of Bill Copperwaith had set the bar for yurts back in the 70s. Some argue this guy is the father of yurts in North America. He also happened to live in Downeast Maine and sold plans to build the hard sided yurt he designed. "What the heck," I told Autumn as I sent away for a set. "Let's see how hard it is."

Several weeks later while I was boiling down maple sap to make syrup over a campfire, the mail arrived with the plans. I was not really pleased. The plans were more a rough sketch of a madman with no actual rhyme or reason as to the procedure to build. They were better to frame and display than to build. It was at this point my ambition to actually construct one waned.

The hard sided yurt plans were just one symptom of a spring that required change. We'd worked out a lot of kinks in our first twelve months. The need to live adjacent to my folks to test run our strange house was gone. We were free to move. We wanted to move. We just needed to find where.

My parents were looking at a 50-acre woodlot a mile away while we were looking around ourselves. I dreamt of a nice wooded spot, preferably next to a stream. The prospect of another summer suffering in the heat was far too much to bear. We needed options.

Adding to the desire to move, my spring cleaning of the yurt revealed wear. The sun had faded the green sides. Heat and sunlight caused the para-cord that kept the valance secured over the sidewalls to break. The repair wasn't expensive but seemed excessive considering the yurt wasn't a year old. I tied the broken edges together as a temporary fix.

The Velcro surrounding the front two windows was the worst damage though. Sun bleached, sections no longer stuck. Which meant the plastic windows didn't attach fully. These were the two windows with the awning kits installed. Despite trying to protect the windows, damage had occurred. Now if we attached the plastic outer pieces halfway down to allow air flow through the top, a good gust of wind could rip the outer covers away. We'd find them blown off the deck when we came home after a run to the grocery store.

The Velcro needed repair, but with half of it attached to the actual side of our house, it was a problem without a good immediate solution. Just like our desire to move.

The tan frame around each window is the Velcro which attaches the plastic cover to the screened opening in the yurt wall

With the change in seasons and spring cleaning, we found another problem. Autumn released two mice into the yurt! Extra bins of lighter clothing as well as stored kitchen items that Autumn wanted now that she had an indoor oven and better counters had been stored in the under-yurt room she'd built. Though it had nice walls and even a window to help vent the battery gas, it was a dirt floor basement-like room. I'd put down interlocking anti-fatigue mats that I'd once had in our garage at the old house as a flooring. But without a solid floor and walls built around deck support posts, the space was hardly critter-tight.

A few opportunistic mice made their way into the storage area over the winter. And two managed to slip into a bin that had a lid imperfectly snapped on. Autumn brought up that bin one night to sort through. She popped the lid, picked it up and out jumped two mice. The dogs were thrilled! I was not.

A hunt by all family members ensued. I managed to catch one in an upside down bowl and relocated it outside. The other Autumn chased into the bathroom where it disappeared. After a long fruitless search, it became too dark to find anything in the yurt despite wearing camping headlamps. We gave up. The mouse never turned up and after a few days, we assumed that it slipped out the sidewall between the screws holding down the outside cover to the platform.

With spring coming on we could not stand by and avoid doing the things that we loved such as gardening and enjoying the spring weather despite the problems cropping up. The gardens were uncovered, leaves raked aside, frames fixed, and plans for new plants made.

— Adam

ONE YEAR
JUNE 2011

*"So many people ask me what we'll do when we get old.
'I mean is the yurt for the rest of your lives?'*

*I had thought our first house was for the rest of my life.
When we sold it a year and a half later, I thought surely our
second house was for forever. Then we sold it for the yurt. I
don't really know what I'll be doing or where I'll be ten years
from now or five or two or really even one. No one does. We
all think we do but it can change in one instant, with one
decision.*

*What I say is 'Nah, I'm saving up for a 32-foot
sailboat.'"*

\- Autumn: 4 June 2011

A dam hit up the seedling sale first. He had my wish list and his, and did the best he could with what was available. He reported that the local hardware store had the best selection and price on herbs, even though that meant not buying locally. With most of the garden plants from area farms, I caved in for the herbs: cheap and plentiful over local. At least I was supporting a locally owned store.

Even after Adam's purchases were planted and then a handful I added to the garden, there was one gap. It took some thinking to figure out what we could possibly put in the one-foot by three-foot prime garden real estate. We wanted something that would provide more than one meal, but couldn't have anything like carrots due to the depth of the beds. Finally I had an idea.

"Brussels sprouts! You get multiple meals from one plant, they grow upright so they don't take much room, and they'll last until late fall as we'll get to use them for a long time."

It was a good idea with one problem. We couldn't find any brussel sprout seedlings. I put the idea aside and tried to come up with another solution. Until Adam swung by my office one day on his motorcycle.

"You'll never guess what I have in the tank bag."

I tried a few random guesses but was completely stumped. He unzipped the bag to show a series of tiny green plants.

"Brussels sprouts."

"Where did you get them?"

It turned out that a small roadside stand had six plants. He'd been on the bike, but had managed to find a way to transport the small seedlings snuggled in the tank bag. By the time I got home, they were planted and the garden was complete.

Our first year was over too. June 4th marked one year from the first day of construction. June 6th would make it one year since it had been complete. At least finished on the exterior. I'd only installed the new oven and counter top in March. Inside, the yurt was still transforming.

Outside we were creating adaptations as well. Adam unrolled the window covers secured above the back two windows. With some folding and clipping of snaps and a bit of tying off to close stationary objects, he created two shades that could funnel water into an old oak barrel for the one and the rain barrel for the other. For the first time, we could actually capture rain water for the shower like we'd envisioned over a year before.

"I can't believe we were going to spend over $100 each on two awnings when it took you an hour and some rope to come up with something better."

Adam grinned. "Yeah, but the awnings work well on the front because we can see out of them better."

"True. Either way at least we can keep the plastic window covers off even if it rains now."

We did not mark the yurt turning one year old. No belated yurt warming party; no wine or beer toasted to round homes. Instead, we enjoyed the deck once again. Adam rigged an old sail into an artistic shade cover across the front of the yurt. It helped keep the front door that faced the blazing sun a few degrees cooler, which helped lower the temperature in the yurt as well.

We bought an actual outdoor table with umbrella for the deck. The tiny folding table of the year before had worked, but there was something nice about a real table and sun shade. Finally we had a shady spot for lunch when the sun was blazing down eating shadows to tiny slivers.

Ants drove us crazy. The year before the yurt had been new as well as the deck. Not a critter had disturbed us other than the biting and flying sort. This spring a few large ants and hundreds of tiny ones trailed a line up the deck. The little ones Adam identified as acrobat ants. They would surround the outside of the yurt before venturing in near the door. My greatest fear was they would find the highly ant-insecure icebox.

With two dogs, pesticides were a dangerous choice. Adam found the ant colony living, or at least stopping, at a stump ten feet from the yurt before coming up a ramp I had constructed for easy off-deck access to the wood pile. He apologized before ripping the ramp from the deck. It took a few days, but the ants finally found both the steps and a good path up the deck supports. We used diatomaceous earth wherever we could. Adam contemplated ways of removing the infected stump.

The larger ants were less of a problem, being random foragers. I found it best to keep my cereal in Tupperware. Most other kitchen items were already in glass jars. It was really just the acrobat ants that were driving us batty. With fabric walls that screwed to the platform lip at a two-foot interval, they could meander in anywhere they chose. So much for my peaceful yurt dreams of living contentedly in nature.

Even though the ants were pushing us to war, I kept my happiness at yurt living. It was a choice and I no longer felt the need to apologize for it. I no longer stumbled when I told work associates I lived in a yurt and yes, it is like a giant tent. To those curious enough, I would describe the antique fridge, the outhouse, and the solar system.

Very few people were taken aback. Though our vet made the comment we were awfully clean for people who lived in a yurt. I didn't know how to take the remark. We still washed our clothes on a regular basis, only now we used a laundromat instead of a rather old and tired washer and drier in a basement. I showered every night. I think our puzzled expressions must have shown, but she did suggest the cheapest alternatives possible for pet health care. Obviously she felt yurt dwellers were dirty and poor.

Those presumptions were few. The more people I told I lived in a yurt, the more yurt dwellers or former yurt dwellers I met. We included anyone living in a small off-grid space as allies and swapped ideas, solutions, and innovations. Having a creative streak seemed to either be a necessity or a learned trait for anyone living unconventionally.

One of the concepts that I did find strange was that we were living "simply." On one level, I understood what this meant. We were living closer to nature. But really there was nothing simple about it. This lifestyle was more complex to the end user. Adam and I spent hours figuring out solutions to such things as heat, water, food storage, and bathroom arrangements. Sometimes it took hours of work to make things function. Flipping a switch to turn on a light, or twisting a faucet for water is simple.

What it did provide was an appreciation for necessities that we'd once taken for granted. And beyond the essentials, anything else was a luxurious treat. I could thrill Adam in the summer by bringing home ice. Going for ice cream was an event. A warm yurt on a raw New England day was a joy. It defined home.

Life was a series of days with immediate experiences. If we were hot, we went for a swim. If it was cold, we added wood to the fire. If we wanted to live better, we needed to innovate a solution to solve whatever was causing a problem. Improvements were felt immediately and were usually for something highly important. We learned to cut a lot of the unnecessary time-wasting crap from our lives along with the extra possessions. This was life streamlined to what was important and then focusing on those things so you didn't take it for granted. The simple part really meant that: cutting the clutter and living aware of the day around you.

It was a night in mid-June as Adam and I sat out on the deck by our new table that we began to discuss the year ahead.

"I want to do something about the icebox. I don't want to deal with the ice and slime mold again this summer," he said.

"Okay, what do you think?"

"What about one of those really insulated coolers?"

I frowned. "Maybe. I really want to get a composter this year. It bothers me not to be able to compost the tea leaves and coffee grounds."

Adam nodded. The list continued. We needed to do something about the rain that could force its way under the French doors, much less freezing them shut in the winter, as well as the heat loss.

"Maybe storm doors?"

And we could improve the insulation Adam had made for the top dome. The outhouse could use a few items too, now that it was the permanent solution.

"I think we should get a wind turbine before winter. The highest winds are on the cloudy days, so we could charge without the sun."

The between rafter support kitchen shelves installed later that summer

161

"That is a good idea. How much does that cost?"

Adam shrugged. "A small wind generator ... I'll have to look into it."

"Otherwise, we could see if we can reduce energy somewhere," I suggested. "And I hate the jelly cabinet in the kitchen. I think I want to build shelves between the rafter supports in there."

"Sounds good."

We both smiled. Now that we'd been through one year in the yurt, the next one was going to be that much better.

— Autumn

"Apparently blowing up a stump with black powder does not work the way they show in the movies."

\- Adam: 6 June 2011

A dapt and Overcome, that is the necessary thing to think, say, and commit to when trying to live in a yurt or any off-grid arrangement. Such a lifestyle takes perseverance and the difficulties are vast. Though the rewards are worth the struggle. During our year we found that every day presented a great challenge. Each challenge had to be met with a innovative solution. Some solutions had to be delayed or even modified as the days progressed.

During our year in the yurt we came to see life in a much different light. We saw that life was fluid. The norm is not always right. We realized that people will judge you no matter what you do, where you live, or how you dress. We both grew as a result of living there. We learned to mellow out. Stewart the rat can have our old house. While I still disliked him, I feel that he got the karma he deserved: a cold, leaky insulator from nature. The transition from a regular house to the yurt was hard but turned out for the best.

The more I looked at the yurt, the more I disliked the amount of wear I saw in our home and the more I found. There was more than what a single year of living there should have caused. The sun had taken its toll on the stitching. I'd been focused on the window Velcro, but when I found that not only the loops were damaged, but the thread holding it on, I started inspecting the rest of the sidewall. Other sections had broken threads. The yurt looked the way I'd expect after five years of hard living. We could buy a new sidewall. I'd read of others who switched between a summer light color and a winter dark. But it would be a big expense, at least $5,000, which was far too much for something that appeared to be almost a yearly maintenance need.

A good day where I roasted coffee beans on the wood stove

Then the ants made their way into the yurt from god knows where. One or two insects, I can handle. But a thousand insects circling the outside perimeter to slip into the yurt at any point was too much. I hate pesticides, especially having small dogs and loving spiders, snakes, birds, really the environment. There is a line of thought, too, about what could be allowed to enter the house. An ant colony sharing the space was too much. We did what we could as naturally as we could. I tried to stop the problem before it reached the deck by removing easy access onto the platform and then by blowing up the stump where the ants seemed to be stopping.

Everything I tried only set them back a day or so before they found a solution. Even the diatomaceous earth, which worked well to slow them down from climbing up the deck posts, needed to be replaced after every rain or heavy dew. As if the ants knew that, they would scurry up the posts en masse after each rain or during the early morning. I half expected to see them making a path by carting away each piece of the dust.

All the problems required a big brainstorming session. We made plans to improve our situation, including possible wind power, shading ideas, and even the idea of picking up the yurt for a move!

— Adam

EPILOGUE
YEARS 2, 3 AND BEYOND.
MAY 9, 2016

"Everyone I know who has lived in a yurt builds a cabin before the end of year three."

- Dave M. 2011

T he irony is that we faced the fact that the yurt wasn't working a month after we paid off the loan that had helped us purchase it. We'd attained our goal. We were debt free and had a place to live. But the place was getting beat to heck and we had little peace being so close to Adam's parents. We needed separation and that meant moving. But the yurt was moveable, right?

I didn't relish the idea of taking it down. Lifting the roof had nearly cost Adam his back. Taking it down and putting it back up again, somewhere else ...? Plus the circular platform would have to be identical in size for the snow load supports to fit. I couldn't make them longer unless I bought more wood.

But taking it down did create some potential benefits. We'd done our best to create a functional interior during the two years we'd lived in it while combating ants and a chickadee that enjoyed attacking our shiny chimney while driving Adam insane in the process. The chickadee was easy, a super soaker slowed him down. The ants ... were a constant summer problem.

Beyond that, the bathroom wedge was bigger than it needed to be if we didn't have a composting toilet. And I had to agree with Adam, grudgingly. The yurt lost a bit of tranquility with this large object carving out a section. Then the kitchen wasn't quite what I'd envisioned. I made it work, but I had planned on nicer shelves, and a better counter. The small shelves between the roof supports along the outside wall worked but were made with salvaged wood and brackets. They held lots of essentials, but I won't say I liked them.

And the floor ... our biggest mistake was that we hadn't put down a decent floor, even linoleum, over the plywood before putting up the snow load supports. We'd painted the plywood, but it wasn't wearing well and was impossible to clean. Moving the yurt offered a lot of potential to fix mistakes that we hadn't realized were mistakes until too late.

But where?

We started looking around for wooded lots. Moving out of the sun and its potent summer heat, hot enough to melt candles in the yurt, was a priority. But cheaper lots in Maine meant a swamp. Then we found a site that we absolutely fell for. Twenty-five acres with a stream and some frontage on a lake, the land rolled with little wet hollows perfect for cranberries or elderberries up to rocky highs topped with towering hemlock trees. We were in love.

And that is when we found out there was someone else equally in love. That same week several home loan companies informed us they did not provide loans for land. Maybe they would consider a construction loan for a house lot, which they considered five acres maximum. Oh, and a yurt wouldn't count as a house for construction.

The news stymied us until we learned about potentially getting a farm loan. We launched into creating a farm and forest business plan based on permaculture practices plus constructing a couple of rental cabins. The cabins were awfully cute. At the same time, we put in a bid for the lot, and then another until we were in a full-out bidding war. The price skyrocketed to something that would have us paying a mortgage for a good thirty years. It is amazing how quickly life choices can spiral beyond where you were intending to go. We'd be tied to this land, land that we loved, trying to make a go of it farming instead of traveling. I'd need to keep my day job a lot longer.

We lost the bid on the land a few days before the new bank turned down the business plan needed for the farm loan. We were heartbroken. I was a little relieved.

We still had nowhere to go.

And then Adam's parents offered to let us move the yurt to a small woodlot a mile away from where it was located. We walked the land and looked at options. It was pretty. It didn't have any streams but did have a spring so we were hopeful we could find water. The nicest spots had huge pine trees with massive branches. The sort of limbs that would drop straight through a fabric yurt roof. We kept looking.

We also took a closer look at the yurt. Some of the windows hadn't been sticking well the fall before. Two summers in the sun with frequent adjustments on and off during fall weather as well as the furious storms of August had worn the Velcro to fuzz. Three of them really needed mending. The door too looked worn. The rough storm doors Adam had made helped prevent freezing and improved the warmth over the winter. But they, too, needed repair, especially if we wanted to change them to screen doors for the fast approaching summer.

You know, those cabins were really cute.

We found a perfect spot to build and decided it would be a cabin. Construction began in 2012 with a design we created. I never would have tackled building a house if we hadn't built so much for the yurt. If we hadn't built the yurt.

Keeping in mind our struggles, one of the first things accomplished was drilling a well and installing a hand pump. Now gathering water meant driving to the cabin site and filling gallon jugs. We had as much water as we wanted and I felt rich. By December 2012, a mild one thank goodness, we had the outside of the cabin complete. In February, we began insulating. By spring we were full into drywall.

During the spring of 2013, we came home with a used propane fridge and freezer and I wondered why I had resisted one earlier. It was awesome. We had ice cream and cold beer whenever we liked! The simplest pleasures are still the best. There was nothing like coming back to the yurt after a day building the house to take a hot shower and drink something cold.

Using a hand pump to get water in winter is hard, but not nearly as bad as melting snow

As the summer of year three in the yurt baked, we spent more time building the cabin and listed the yurt. It sold to a local farmer who wanted it for seasonal help. It was a sad and happy sale. We moved into the house before it was fully complete so the yurt could be taken down before fall.

No longer would we feel the breeze as the walls breathed with the wind or hear the faintest rain misting the roof. It was a difficult separation. But our first winter in the cabin was the coldest in Maine for years. To make up for the yurt's lack of insulation, we stuffed the cabin full. The tiny wood stove that had heated the yurt but needed replenishing every three hours on the coldest nights heated the entire cabin overnight. I could sleep eight hours straight.

Still off-grid and now needing to snowmobile to the main road where we parked the cars, winter in the cabin was more isolated than the yurt had been. It was warmer too. And unlike the yurt, we designed it to be closed up and left. So if the option to travel came around, we'd be able to walk away and come back without worrying about ants in the kitchen and a branch through the roof. Or like the one winter trip we'd taken, a frozen pipe in the instant hot water heater used for the shower that required repairs.

A friend told me that everyone they knew who lived in a yurt built a cabin by year three. Oddly, a few other yurt dwelling friends started cabin construction around the same time we did.

The yurt wasn't a mistake. It was an adventure. I learned so much about myself, about living in nature, about what we really need to live and be happy. I miss its breezy sighs and want a small yurt; not for day-to-day living, but for a writer's cabin or a retreat. It would be a special place that signifies the peace you feel in one. A place you can stay when the weather isn't so harsh as to require thermal underwear while the wood stove is glowing because you have it burning so hot. A place that won't mean panic if something does rip the side or a window falls off. Because it isn't the only housing option.

Adam recently said if he built another yurt, he'd build it over a garage. That way you'd have storage below, a place for the bathroom, shower, plumbing, and wood stove. While the upstairs could be a yurt in its perfect roundness, heated from below with warm floors. I think he might be on to something there.

We've had the cabin three years now and itchy feet is setting in. I love it. Adore it. But I no longer look at decisions as unalterable, set in stone, permanent choices. The world is a big place and my journey isn't finished yet.

— Autumn

"Honestly Dad, this is our house. What the hell were you thinking kicking a basketball into our sidewall?"

- Adam, August 10th 2011

"Why are you looking at land to move the yurt to? Just build it on our land up the hill."

- Adam's Parents, March 15th 2012

The summer of 2011 went by hotter than the first year. Much of our time was spent in the shade on the far side of the yurt. The ATVs became more present and the ant problem increased. Our second year was turning out to be much more difficult than the first.

We also discovered that the yurt was not holding up very well in the constant sun. The fabric was loosening and the stitching was breaking down. Our door was beginning to delaminate and the plastic was crazing. Some rot was found in the floor as well. It was decided that we had a few options: sell the yurt and move while it was still worth something, move the yurt to a location out of the sun and address the issues, or finally sell the yurt and build a cabin on my parents' land. All options were carefully considered and in the end we decided on the cabin route.

So why did we give up the yurt? Did we grow tired of the hardships? Was it worth the money?

We chose what we did because we saw the yurt depreciating very fast. While we still had equity we could sell it and build something that would last more than ten years. Heck, it should last more than three. Our dream when we started out was to be more mobile and to start out on new adventures. The yurt was actually holding us back.

We could not heat it sufficiently or cool it. It had to be tended. We could not have it in the open as it would get too hot, could not have it in the woods as a tree would crush it ... the yurt was a constant worry that kept us tied. The cabin allowed us a more solid place that could be left for years. Trees would not destroy it. We could winterize the structure and not be stuck dealing with any number of disasters instead of heading off. It was also cheaper to heat and easier to stay cool.

The newly installed wind turbine next to the solar panel – we removed the deck railings to leverage the pole into place using the tech-no-post originally installed for the panel

Living in the yurt was a wonderful experience, but between living so close to my parents which were taking as much advantage of me as we them, the relationship became strained. We had to get out of there and the yurt had to come down.

We ended selling the yurt for $8000 after paying about $15000 in total and lived there for about two and a half years. I am a bit biased about value and in some ways the yurt was a good deal but

173

in other ways, especially the accessories, I felt gouged on the pricing. The quality of the yurt could have been better and with some damage caused in shipping, the company did not make the it right by sending a new part for the door or giving us a credit. Many of the accessories we designed and made cheaply, they sold for a very high price and for those reasons I have never recommended them.

Taking down the yurt was relatively easy. We let the buyers disassemble. We figured it was easier for them to do it so they'd know how it went up. The deck, however, was a nightmare. It was timber frame and not built as we had requested, to be easily disassembled, but as a permanent structure. What should have taken two weekends took a good part of the summer. As an interesting side note, upon taking a chainsaw to the former yurt floor beneath both the door and the shower stall I unearthed a colony of about 10,000,000 acrobat ants. In another part I found a nest of carpenter ants. I guess I finally figured out the ant problem!

We still have much of our deck in pieces, now near our cabin. I do miss the yurt. It's dryness and outside feel. I miss it whenever I think of it. There are no regrets for having lived in one, and I hope someday to actually own another smaller one … just so the next one does not have a disruptive wedge in the middle!

— Adam

See the book photos online!

Visit http://www.nomapnomad.com/a-year-in-a-yurt-photos/ to access all of the photos in the book, and even a few I left out to save space!

Are You a Homesteader?

Or a yurt dweller, prefer wilderness to urban, live in a tiny or micro-home, or any of the above? Or just wish you did? Great! Join us on Facebook in our Homesteading and Wilderness Living Group at https://www.facebook.com/groups/Homesteadtoday where we problem solve with a bit more brain power than going it alone! And since you just read the book, I'd love to know what you think. See you there!

— Autumn

ABOUT AUTUMN RAVEN

Autumn (also known as Weifarer and Autumn M. Birt) is a travel and fiction writer currently based in Maine where she lives in a small cottage lost in the woods, which she built with her husband and with the supervision (and approval) of two Cairn terriers.

With a Bachelor of Arts degree from Bucknell University in Studio Arts and English, Autumn once considered a career in illustration. However, an ecology course at Virginia Tech led to a Master of Science degree in Ecology and Environmental Sciences from the University of Maine in Orono. After graduation with her M.S., Autumn has worked for the USDA Natural Resources Conservation Service. This was a great job that not only let her help the environment and protect local agriculture, but also gave her a paycheck big enough to support her writing habit until finally ... at long last she is now a full time writer and on-line educator!

You can learn more about Autumn's books and writing courses online at her website www.AutumnWriting.com including her latest work-in-progress. If you want to get an automatic email when

Autumn's next book is released, sign up here. Your email address will never be shard and you can unsubscribe at any time.

Word of mouth is crucial for any author to succeed. If you enjoyed the book, please consider leaving a review where you purchased it, or on Goodreads, even if it's only a line or two; it would make all the difference and would be very much appreciated.

Connect with Autumn Online:

Twitter: http://twitter.com/weifarer
Facebook:
https://www.facebook.com/Author.Autumn.Birt
Amazon: http://www.amazon.com/Autumn-M.-Birt/e/B007B2AFCS
Blogs: http://www.AutumnWriting.com
http://NoMapNomads.com
http://www.escapewiththedog.com/

ABOUT ADAM RAVEN

Adam is a Wilderness Guide, Fishing Guide, college professor and conservation photographer who has spent a good part of his life in the woods and field of the northeast from Martha's Vineyard to the Gaspe' He has traveled from Peru to Alaska and love to experience the natural world as much as he can. He is often joined by his dog Ayashe and wife Autumn Birt Raven.

His primary focus is on the awareness, preservation and photographic documentation of the environment. From a young age he was brought up with a closeness and spiritual connection to the natural world. His desire to protect what he holds dear resonates in his guiding and photography classes, for the entire purpose of his passion is to show people what he sees himself, that we are not separate from the environment...but very much part of it.

He is also a Wilderness first responder, Pet First Responder, licensed pilot, scuba diver and has been educated in forestry, conservation law and Aquatic resources.

Connect with Adam Online:

Twitter: https://twitter.com/AdamRavenGuide
Facebook:
https://www.facebook.com/Raventography/
Websites: http://NoMapNomads.com
http://www.theravengallery.com/
Blog: http://www.escapewiththedog.com/

Made in the USA
Middletown, DE
14 December 2018